CHURCHES
SERVING
SCHOOLS

DAVID W. LANKSHEAR

The National Society (Church of England) for
Promoting Religious Education

The National Society
Church House
Great Smith Street
London SW1P 3NZ

ISBN 0 901819 49 2

Published 1996 by The National Society/Church House Publishing

Printed in England by Bourne Press Ltd

Contents

Introduction

A resource book for the Churches
on their relationships with schools

The telephone rang in the parish priest's study. 'Hello, my name is Brown. I am head teacher of Gasworks Road Primary School. I see that you have a flag flying on the church today. One of my pupils says that he sings in your choir and that he thinks that the flag is flying because it's something called Ascension Day. Could you give me some more information so that I can answer the children's questions?'

Like many of the examples in the pages that follow, this is a report of a real incident (although the names have been changed). It seems sad that the head teacher of the local primary school and the parish priest of the local Anglican church did not know each other. At least the head teacher in this story had picked up the telephone to ask the question. This could provide the start of something good for both school and church.

This book is for all involved in local ministry in the Christian Churches. It provides a guide to the schools in the education system of England and Wales and contains a range of suggestions on the ways in which good relations may be developed between Churches and the schools in the area that they serve.

It sets out to raise some pertinent questions and to share some suggestions and experiences of how the relationships may be developed in practice. The book is divided into four parts. The first part will consider some of the theoretical questions. The second part will establish some definitions and describe some key aspects of the school system and Church organisation. It is assumed that most readers will benefit from a study of one but not both of these parts. Some whose ministerial role is combined with professional knowledge of the education system may decide to skip both.

The third and longest part deals with the practical issues and seeks to identify what schools and Churches can do. There are many suggestions and no one school or church is likely to try them all. Everything suggested has happened recently or is happening now somewhere in England or Wales.

Local communities often assume that their churches and schools are capable of working together. This assumption is not always shared by the staff of the schools or those in leadership roles in the churches. They may see problems and difficulties where the community seems to see only opportunities and traditions.

One of my assumptions in preparing this book is that the Christian Church is not just a group of people who share the same beliefs, nor is it just a worshipping community, although it should be both of these. I assume that the Church is also a group of people who take action for, within or on behalf of the wider community in which they meet. The Church's involvement in such action is usually good for the wider community, and it is certainly good for individual Christians and the churches that they attend. Therefore, this book provides a variety of suggestions for action and these are discussed in the fourth part.

The key questions underlying the book are:

- Why should the Christian Church seek to develop good relationships with the schools in the area which it serves?

- Why should a school welcome good relations with the Churches in the area from which it draws its pupils?

- How may Churches and schools best work together?

In preparing this book I am grateful to the numerous priests, ministers and teachers, who, by sharing their work with me over the years, have contributed to it. Theirs is the good work. The errors and failures in describing it are mine.

I am also grateful to Daphne Griffith, Alan Brown and Leslie Francis for their comments on various drafts of the text.

Part I

THE BACKGROUND

1

Why should Churches serve schools?

T here are many possible answers to the question posed by the title of this chapter. Sometimes the question is phrased in terms of priorities as in this quotation from the elderly childless church council member.

> I don't know why our priest spends so much time in that school. If he didn't keep popping in there for cups of coffee perhaps he'd have more time to visit church members in their homes. We have to pay for him after all.

It is a good point. It goes to the heart of Christian ministry. Our priests and ministers cannot do everything in the church. There must be priorities. Members of the congregation should contribute their time, their energies and their talents to the work of the church. Even if they do so regularly and generously, it is still not possible for the churches to do all the things that are desirable. Many Churches are finding difficulty in sustaining the number of paid priests, ministers or workers that was accepted as normal even a generation ago. Many church members find it ever more difficult to commit time to voluntary Christian service. Choices need to be made. Why should work in schools figure importantly in the priorities of Churches? Should it take priority over the flower rota or sending relief to disaster areas? Why should Churches serve schools?

There are many possible answers to these questions. In order to stimulate thought and discussion a number of possible answers are offered in the following pages. These answers are described in terms of the approaches which are adopted by some local churches or church members to the churches' relationship with schools. In many churches individual members of the church will adopt one or more of these viewpoints and sometimes a completely different view from any described here. In areas where there is more than one church, the Churches may differ in their styles and policies in relation to the schools in that location. The views selected and described here are designed to stimulate thought and discussion; they are not intended to be an exhaustive list. Sixteen models of answers have been identified as follows:

1. The Mallory
2. The Anglican
3. The domestic
4. The mutual interest
5. The traditional
6. The consumer
7. The biblical
8. The industrial
9. The 'open all hours'
10. The shrine
11. The evangelical
12. The witness
13. The provider
14. The supporter
15. The young family
16. The older generation

1. The Mallory or 'Because they are there'

George Lee Mallory (1886-1924) was a famous mountaineer before the Second World War. When he was asked why he climbed mountains he replied, 'Because they are there.' For many, this may be the level at which the response to the question posed above is answered. Will it suffice as a response for church people who are looking ever more carefully at how time is used by priests, ministers and lay members of the church? Therefore, Churches are forced to review their priorities. For some church people the response to a review will be simply that the existence of schools in the area around the church presents so many opportunities for service in the name of Christ that this alone is sufficient reason to justify the time spent. Others may need more convincing when they can identify many other conflicting claims on time and resources.

2.   The Anglican or 'The cure of souls'

When Anglican priests are inducted into a new parish they are told that they are given 'the cure of souls' in the parish. This is to make it clear that they have a responsibility for everyone in the parish, not just those who attend church. This commitment to the parish as a whole is, at the same time, the strength and weakness of so many Anglican churches. It is a strength when it leads to selfless service to the community in the name of Christ, or when as a result it provides contact points for those who are searching, but have yet to find faith. It is weak when membership must be defined to justify requests for support from outside bodies or to prove that the rumour of the death of the church is exaggerated.

In relation to schools the 'Anglican' response argues that, if the parish priest is responsible for everyone in the parish, he or she must be concerned with the schools within that parish. It does not matter whether there are any church members in the school; that is not the point. The school is in the parish, that is all that is necessary to justify the time spent by the priest or other members of the church in its service. Those unconvinced will say, 'So are the factory, the shopping centre and the sewage farm. Why should schools be high on the list?'

3.   The domestic or 'concern for "our" children'

The 'domestic' response focuses attention on the members of the church community, children or adult, who are also involved in the school. 'Our' children are being taught in these schools. 'Our' people are working in them. The church wishes to maintain contact and to become involved because of its care for its members. Such a proper concern to understand, to support and to share mutual commitments to children and adults may sometimes be misinterpreted by schools. Taken to extremes, schools may respond as if they interpret such approaches as coming from a pressure group. Church members need to ensure that their approach is along the lines of 'I would like to talk to you because we share a mutual concern and commitment to these children' and does not stress the negative aspects of the Church's mission to education, e.g. 'I want to talk

5

to you because you are teaching our children and we want to know what you are doing' or even 'I want to let you know that the congregation does not believe that you should be teaching our children . . .'

(The reader is left to use their own experience to fill in the dots.)

Churches adopting the 'domestic' approach are showing the strength of their community and its care for its individual members. They are also providing practical evidence to local schools of the strength of Christian commitment in the area. These are clearly among the merits of such an approach. Those who wish to be critical of the 'domestic' response suggest that it could present the church as inward-looking, concerned principally with its own affairs and they would ask how this is reconciled with the call to evangelism.

4. The mutual interest

We are both groups of concerned people trying to serve this community. We should work together for mutual support and encouragement.

This is much heard in areas where both Churches and schools are under pressure perhaps because the values of both seem to be alien to those of the majority of the community in which they are placed. Taken to extremes, the 'mutual interest' approach could be a sign that both school and church have become alienated from their local community. There are, however, many genuine areas of potential mutual interest and concern. Both churches and schools may share a love of children, a commitment to support parents or an anxiety about the social conditions in the area which they serve. The 'mutual interest' approach may develop very good relationships between the staff of the school and the staff of the church. Work that flows from this can be well founded and of more use to the community than either the local church or school can achieve on their own. It does, however, have the short-coming that it identifies church people and teachers as outside the local community. As a response it can sometimes feel defensive.

5. The traditional or 'We created this system anyway'

The Churches took most of the early initiatives to create a system of schooling in this country that provides education for all. They did this by founding a large number of Church schools during the first 70 years of the nineteenth century. They have not surrendered the task to the State as they have done with so many other welfare and community tasks. There are a number of Churches that are still committed to being part of the education system in this country, not least by maintaining schools within it. The Anglican Church has over 5,000 schools in the maintained system; the Roman Catholic Church over 2,500. While the appeal to historic and continuing involvement is an important justification for Churches to work in schools, there will be many who will wish to know where this is leading and what the Churches' present and future vision is for their involvement in schools.

In different areas, or at different stages of the education system, the particular approach of Church schools may vary. Sometimes the governors of a Church school will make it clear that the first commitment of the school is to provide a Christian education for the children of parents who are members of the denomination that founded the school. In other cases, the governors will state that their first priority is for the school to be of service to the neighbourhood by offering education to the children of all parents living in the area. This service is offered in the name of Christ, and within a school which is endeavouring to be a Christian community. Most Church schools, in practice, combine elements of both these concepts.

Both the Anglican and Roman Catholic Churches have sought to make their vision clear for their own schools, but many members of these Churches have yet to understand fully the reasons behind their denomination's continuing commitment to church schools. (see Chapter 9)

6. The consumer or 'We are as much clients of the system as any employer'

All Churches are dependent on schools for the skills, knowledge and understanding that they teach. Christianity is a literate faith, in that it has a book, the Bible, as one of its foundations. The Bible is used in public worship as well as private study and devotion by most Christians. The Churches assume that most of their members can read with intelligence and discrimination. These skills are usually acquired in schools. In addition, the Churches need well-educated men and women to be its priests, ministers and leaders. Historically, the Churches have provided their own schools and universities to fill this need. To some extent they still continue to do so but in many places the State has taken over the provision. For most church members these are sufficient reasons for Churches to maintain an interest in and commitment to schooling. Others point out that this view puts the Churches alongside other interested consumers such as industry, commerce or the arts whose involvement in schools is less committed if sometimes better focused than the Churches'. Do the Churches wish to find themselves classified as just another consumer group within education?

7. The biblical or 'Working with schools is part of our biblical ministry'

Two gospel passages are often quoted when work with children and young people is discussed in Church contexts. The first describes the incident in which parents brought their children to Jesus and the disciples prevented them. Jesus rebukes his disciples and welcomes the children (Matthew 19. 13-14; Mark 10. 13-16; Luke 18. 15-17). From this incident it is clear that Christ welcomes children into the kingdom. If they are part of the kingdom then the Church should be seeking to serve them and witness to them wherever they are. For many this ministry will be achieved, in part at least, through work in schools.

The second passage is Jesus's threefold challenge to Peter after the resurrection (John 21. 15-19). Biblical scholars may point out that there is little difference in the Greek between the phrase 'feed my lambs' and the phrase 'feed my sheep', both apparently intended to indicate that Peter was being given a pastoral charge for the people of God. Those who have a strong commitment to children, however, seek to make more of the difference. They point out that it was one of the leading apostles that was given the charge to 'feed my lambs'. They argue from this that today's Church leaders locally and nationally should follow Peter and accept their responsibility to give time and attention to work among children and young people.

As schools become more demanding of pupils' time and commitments, it is not surprising that many Church leaders are seeking to work with and in schools in their commitment to this aspect of their ministry.

8.   The industrial or 'Education is a major employer and we should offer chaplaincy in the work place'

Education is a major industry. Over eight million people work in the education industry, but not all of these are paid, of course. There are the teachers and the support staff. There are the governors, the administrators, the advisers and the inspectors. The largest number of people working in the education industry are, however, the children and students themselves.

> What do you mean attending school is work? They only seem to play these days and anyway some of them like school so it cannot be hard work.

Ask any student working for GCSE or watch a group of young children wrestling with a problem and you will discover how hard the work can be. Enjoying what they are doing and working hard are not incompatible.

Education is indeed a major industry, carried out in small or large units in every community in the country. The Churches provide a service of specialist chaplains for hospitals, the armed forces and manufacturing, distribution and marketing industries. Within this model work undertaken by Churches in schools is another form of industrial chaplaincy. There are already some people who are identified as chaplains to schools, particularly independent schools, to further education colleges and to universities. They could find their work more valued by the church if this model were to be more widely adopted. Some church members will argue, however, that this model is dangerous because children and young people are not doing 'paid' work at school and that the industrial chaplaincy model may tend to emphasise the relationship and care that the

Churches should have with the staff of the schools rather than the pupils. Even if this is a weakness of the approach, the 'industrial' does serve to emphasise the scale and importance of the challenge.

9.   The 'open all hours' or 'We have a wonderful building and schools are welcome to visit us'

This approach has its roots in the importance to the community and the quality of the church buildings. In Churches adopting this approach the building is an important meeting place – the focus of the local Christian community. Part of the mission strategy of such Churches is to encourage people to come in. Therefore, being open and accessible is a key part of their approach. At one extreme the great cathedrals with their visitor centres, bookshops and tea rooms are part of this tradition but so are the humble churches that strive to stay open all day despite the risks of theft and vandalism. Such churches will wish to create opportunities for schools to visit them. They will wish every local child to feel at ease and familiar with their building and will see encouraging school visits as an important part of this strategy.

Churches working in this way will be familiar with what is discussed in later sections of this book about preparing for school visits (see page 57). They will also be ready with their answer to the critics who suggest that this approach places the church on a par with the local museum and concert hall as places to visit and use which have no other important functions. In towns where redundant churches have been converted to such community uses, the criticism will have an added dimension. How do churches that have a well-developed ministry to visitors ensure that the prime purpose of the building as a place of worship is known and valued by all?

10.   The shrine or 'We have a wonderful building that is so holy that schools may visit us on certain conditions'

For some churches their building, or part of it, is such a 'holy' place that they feel uncomfortable and concerned about visitors, especially children, who may not know the rules, coming in and disturbing the character and atmosphere. They will put a great deal of effort into preparing their church to receive visitors and helping visitors to prepare themselves for their visits. Their members, who receive the visitors, will also be there to ensure that such visitors do not offend the rules and tradition. In many such churches there will be occasions during the year when the story of the 'shrine' and the place or things with which it is associated are celebrated. These occasions or records of them may provide a special opportunity to communicate some of the most important aspects of the faith.

These churches' commitment to careful preparation and the maintenance of a worshipful atmosphere may make visits by children and young people a particularly important part of their spiritual development. Without such a commitment to help with preparation for a visit the 'shrine' approach can amount to putting a padlock on the gate and erecting large signs saying 'No entry – members only'.

11. The evangelical or 'We must preach the Good News in schools'

Many Churches will be quick to recognise and own this approach. The Churches must present Christ to this generation of children in order to win them to the faith. This is a clear task of all the Christian Churches (see, for example, 2 Corinthians 4. 1-6). Is it, however, the best motivation for the Churches' relationship with schools? Schools are places where meaning is explored and truth pursued in a safe environment, or at least they should be. Unless it is a Church school, work in the classroom about Christianity will be designed to enable pupils to understand what Christians believe and what it might mean to be a Christian. In many Church schools this will still be a strong theme. Some Church schools, however, may also be able to make the assumption that their pupils are being brought up within Christian homes and thus present some aspects of their teaching about Christianity as learning about a shared faith.

There may be times when a church's commitment to evangelism and a school's concern for education about religion come into conflict. An example of this could arise when pupils need opportunities to explore with Christians what it means to them to be Christian. To be invited to attend a school to help students with this exploration is a privilege. To seek to use that invitation to challenge the pupils to make their own decision for Christ is to abuse the hospitality. Such challenges should be presented, but outside the school context and in places to which the children or young people have come voluntarily and perhaps even knowing that such a challenge will be made.

Some Churches are so committed to the 'evangelical' approach that their representatives would feel unable to talk about their faith without presenting an explicit challenge to their hearers. Such Churches should be open about this in their contacts with schools and only accept invitations to speak in contexts where the presentation of a challenge is appropriate. Some may feel that this limits what they, as a church or an individual, can do in schools and wish to put more energy into serving children and young people outside the school context. This should not prevent them from being involved in developing good relationships with their local schools or showing support for them.

12. The witness or 'We want schools to see Christ in us'

This model draws on the tradition of selfless service which has been part of the Christian commitment down the centuries (see, for example, Matthew 25. 31-40). In serving others, Christians serve Christ. So in serving the schools and the children and adults in them, church members are offering service to their Lord. In making their motives for this service clear, they can make the claims of the gospel attractive. This may lead some to visit our churches or meetings in order to find out more. In visiting schools to explain or make clear what it means to them to be Christians they are also witnessing to the difference that their faith has made. In all of this they provide evidence which can lead others to further exploration.

This commitment is an honourable and continuing tradition within the Churches. It is one that can be easily undervalued in a 'Decade of Evangelism' which some Christians falsely believe is only about the 'Evangelical' approach outlined above. Many Christians who are teaching or working in other capacities in schools as part of their vocation would identify with this approach.

Critics of the approach would question whether the faith is ever made explicit within it. Churches or Christians who approve of this approach should be able to show how a recipient of their service would be able to identify that their motivation is their faith.

13. The provider or 'This church has its own Church school for which it continues to provide financial support'

In provider churches the local congregation has a long-standing commitment to an Aided school. Most of these churches will be Anglican or Roman Catholic. In Aided schools 15 per cent of all the costs of improvements to the buildings and all external repairs must be borne by the governors. The provider church nominates a proportion of the governors and helps the governing body with its costs. The parish priest will almost certainly be a member of the governing body and will give a significant proportion of time each week to work in the school.

Provider churches benefit from having their school. Research shows that they are likely to have more young people and adults involved in their activities than other churches that are not providers (Francis and Lankshear, 1993).

For most provider churches, the school is an important part of their service to the local community. In a few, sadly, where vision has been lost, their schools may be regarded as a drain on church resources. It seems obvious, but it is important to point out that priests or ministers appointed to provider churches should be enthusiastic about the potential role of the school in the parish.

14. The supporter or 'This church has its own Church school but we don't put money into it any more'

Supporter churches have a controlled, a grant maintained (former voluntary) or an independent school with whom they are associated. Unlike provider churches they no longer have to make a financial contribution to the school but they may, through members on the governing body or the trust, have a significant stake in its management. Supporter churches are most likely to be Anglican or Methodist. The priest or minister responsible for the church will be on the governing body and will be active in the school. He/she will probably undertake a regular commitment within the school's programme of worship.

Supporter churches are aware that much effective work is possible with their school if the relationship is good and they will be committed to maintaining such a relationship. Where such good relationships have been maintained over the years, supporter churches may be expected to benefit directly from their involvement in the school. Research results are less certain in this area because the issues are complex and so often affected by local circumstances (Francis, 1987a).

Some churches may have developed such good relationships with county schools and they will recognise their work in this description.

15. The young family or 'We are very concerned about our ministry to children and their families'

These are churches where the majority of the worshippers are under 40, where worship takes account of the presence of children and where it is not uncommon to be welcoming recently born members to the family of the church.

In such congregations local schools will be naturally one of the regular topics of conversation and presumably of prayer. The progress of church children through the schools will be known in general terms. Such churches are well placed to develop good relationships with local schools and also may be able to undertake activities designed to support Christian parents. They have particular experience of worship with children which could be put at the service of local schools.

The most natural starting-point could be the shared responsibility for children between church and school but the danger will always be that this becomes a concern for 'our' children which appears to exclude children not in the congregation.

16. The older generation or 'We don't have any children in our church. Is there any point in our contacting schools?'

Churches where the majority of the congregation is over 50, many having grandchildren, may have some hesitation about their involvement with schools. There are likely to be many members who fear that the presence of children and young people in church will disrupt the quiet, contemplative, worshipful atmosphere which they value.

Churches of this type, however, contain much wisdom and experience which could help schools. They may have members with time and energy which could be made available to schools in their area.

Conclusion

All these models are sustainable, yet all have their drawbacks. Christian Churches and groups at work in the same area may be identifying with different models. Those models that churches feel closest to will, in part, determine the way in which the churches commit time and resources to the school. For example, a church adopting the evangelical model may wish to lead acts of worship in school, while one identifying with the witness model may free a member to serve on the governing body. Where churches in a locality differ about the models that they wish to use and fail to discuss their different perceptions with one another, it is hardly surprising if they seek different types of relationships with local schools. Where this happens schools will receive very mixed messages with which they are unlikely to be able to cope. Churches and individual Christians need to be clearer about the models that they are using and discuss these with each other in order to improve their relationship with local schools.

Points for thought, discussion and action

- How many of the models mentioned in this chapter are supported by members of our church?

- How many are rejected?

- Are the models that are supported mutually compatible?

- Is the same pattern reflected in other churches in our area?

- What messages are we giving to the schools in our area by holding this combination of models?

- Which of these models will schools find attractive?

- Which of these models will schools find threatening?

- What are we going to do about it?

2

What are schools doing?

> You know how it is in schools. You can't mention God or
> Christ. You are not allowed to do anything which suggests
> worship. We had to move our congregation out of the
> school and convert a barn in which to worship.

T he comment recorded above was made to the author with all
the sadness of a gentle Christian soul caught up in a conflict
over the appropriate use of a school building. It will find
much understanding amongst church members who share some of
these perceptions. It will be regarded as unbelievable by those who
know schools. They will be puzzled as to how anyone in this country could so misunderstand what is being attempted in schools.
This chapter is offered to help church people understand more
about what is really happening.

The task

Imagine three people sitting at neighbouring tables in a restaurant.
At the first table is Amy, who speaks five languages and works as an
interpreter for the European Union. She is reading a book on fell
walking. At the next table is Bertha who is involved in the development of the next generation of computers. While she eats her
meal she is listening to a recording of Verdi's *Requiem* on her
Walkman. At the third table is Christine who works as a recep-
tionist for the local doctor. While she is eating she is beginning to
plan the design of her next embroidery project.

For each of these people schools will have provided an important
part of the formal education that has equipped them to do their job
and to follow their leisure interests. Schools have done the same for
the waiter, the cook and all the others involved in the preparation
of their meal. Schools are required to provide an education for
everyone which will prepare them for 'the opportunities, responsibilities and experiences of adult life' (Education Reform Act 1988).

17

It is easy to forget the range of interests and abilities with which a school has to deal. In a class of 29 five-year-olds it may be difficult to discern which child will grow up to be a computer wizard, an artist, a footballer or a waitress – probably none of them. The education that is offered to all the children in the class must take account of and be appropriate for these and many other possibilities.

In the same class of five-year-old children:

- Some of the children will come from homes where both parents are committed readers and books line the walls, while others will have seen adults in their home rarely reading anything but a newspaper or a TV listings magazine.

- Some of the children will have been to nursery school or playgroup every day for the past two years, while others will have remained in their home environment or with a child-minder until entering school.

- Eight of the children are likely to have some contact with a Christian Church and probably three or four with another faith while the majority will have little or no contact with any community of believers.

How do schools approach their task?

The curriculum

All schools in England and Wales must use what the law calls the *Basic Curriculum* as the foundation for their teaching programme. The Basic Curriculum consists of Religious Education with the subjects of the National Curriculum. The National Curriculum subjects are English, mathematics, science, technology, history, geography, art, music, a foreign language (in secondary schools only), physical education and, in Wales, Welsh. The outline and basic content for each of the National Curriculum subjects are developed in England by the School Curriculum and Assessment Agency (SCAA) and approved by the Secretary of State. The Agency also arranges for the assessment of the progress of all schoolchildren at age 7, 11, and 14 through a programme of testing, at age 16 through GCSE and at age 18 through A levels, NVQs and other approved examinations. In Wales this work is undertaken by the Curriculum Council for Wales and approval is given by the Secretary of State for Wales. Individual schools must work within this outline in the production of detailed programmes of work. In addition, every school is inspected every four years against a framework published by The Office for Standards in Education (OFSTED) and related to the National Curriculum. There are equivalent arrangements in Wales for the assessment of pupils' progress and the inspection of schools. These are developed by the office of Her Majesty's Chief Inspector of Schools in Wales.

This pattern of national support created by legislation passed since 1988 still allows freedom for individual schools to choose method-ologies and approaches that suit their own areas and the needs of the children living within them. In this context the unique position of Religious Education is important. Of all the subjects that schools must teach by law, it alone has locally Agreed Syllabuses. For most schools these are developed by the Local Education Authority but for church-aided schools they are often determined by the relevant diocese. The Churches are required to be involved in the process of determining and supporting the Local Education Authority syl-labuses for Religious Education through membership of local Standing Advisory Councils for Religious Education (SACREs) which were established by the Education Reform Act 1988.

The spiritual, moral, social and cultural development of pupils

The Education Act 1996 requires that the school curriculum shall promote: 'the spiritual, moral, cultural, mental and physical devel-opment of pupils at school and of society.' This is achieved in schools by planning a contribution from the programme of teach-ing, the 'hidden curriculum' and school worship. The School Inspection Act 1996 provides for the inspection of these aspects of a school's task and adds social development to the list.

While it is usually assumed that schools understand about the men-tal and physical development of pupils there exists no universally accepted definition of the words 'spiritual, moral, social and cul-tural' in this context. Therefore, it is an area which causes many schools and school inspectors considerable difficulty. A great deal of work is being done to support schools in this work, not least by some of the churches. Policies for each of the four concepts, requiring a contribution from so many areas of a school's life, can be extremely difficult to co-ordinate.

Spiritual development

Christian Churches will have their own understandings of what is meant by spiritual development. Such understandings will vary between Churches in the emphasis they give to private prayer, public worship, service and self-discipline among other aspects of the Christian life. What is a county school with pupils from a number of different faiths to understand by spiritual development when each faith will have its own range of understandings? What does spiritual development mean to those who have no faith? Many schools will adopt a working definition which identifies the spiritual with the emotions and particularly with individuals' responses to the high and low points of human experience. Schools will seek to ensure that there are opportunities for pupils to reflect on their experience at school as part of the process of spiritual education. Also they will wish to teach pupils about the way in which different faiths respond to human experiences and feelings. Christian Churches may be able to resource such work by providing people who can talk about their own spirituality, and by helping schools to plan work in this area. In some instances schools may use the facilities of a church to provide the atmosphere in which pupils can explore contemplation and reflection on their own lives and those of others.

Moral development

A great deal of work has been done on the development of some aspects of moral understanding and behaviour amongst children and young adults. Less has been done to communicate this work to those outside the world of education. Young children first learn the way in which their family does things. When they come to school they may well find that how their family regards certain aspects of behaviour and how school regards it are quite different. This may not be because school and home are opposed but because the circumstances are different. In their early years at school children will be encouraged to learn and abide by the school rules. This learning is usually reinforced by the presence of adults. The aim of such rules must be to help children to learn not only to obey but also to understand the benefits of obeying the rules. Only if this is achieved will children and young people come to accept them for their own sake and therefore obey the rules even when there is no possibility of their being caught breaking them. Teachers working with children towards the later years of primary school will be familiar with this stage of moral learning.

> A dilemma for referees of football matches between primary schools is the advantage rule. In adult games it is accepted that if the rules have been broken but the side offended against wins some benefit from the situation, the referee does not have to take action. He or she can allow the game to proceed. In primary school football if the referee fails to stop the game for each breach of the rules, the game will come to a halt anyway amidst cries of 'it's not fair!'

Later in the development of young people they need to understand that many life situations are too complicated to be solved by the application of simple rules. Within the study of literature or religion there may be many occasions when the question 'Why did he do that?' leads to a moral debate. Here the difference between the rules that a person wishes to live by and the daily dilemmas of living becomes the fundamental stuff of moral education. Within this area the Churches may be able to provide schools with individuals who are able to explain and discuss with young people how their personal faith provides the basis and the strength to resolve such dilemmas. It is unfortunate and at the same time natural that when young people are wrestling with the acceptance for themselves of a standard or faith by which to live, they are most liable to pressure from their peer group. Moral education is not as simple as some would have the public believe, nor does it automatically lead to socially acceptable behaviour – civil disobedience as a way of opposing unjust laws may be a morally appropriate action.

Social development

The first stages of the school's contribution to a child's social development take place in the first few weeks of a child's experience of school. In the family children experience sharing the attention of one or two adults with perhaps one or two other children. Sometimes children will have had the total attention of the adults in their lives. When children arrive at school or playgroup they have to learn to share the attention of the key adults with several other children. They have also to learn to co-operate with the other children in the group. From these early experiences grows an understanding of how to survive in and contribute to the school and, later, society in general. The experience of taking responsibility, raising money for charitable causes, caring for others and participating in making decisions are all aspects of the social development programme which schools provide. In some of these there may be opportunities for schools and their pupils to work in partnership with churches.

Cultural development

In their *Guidance on Inspection of Nursery and Primary Schools,* OFSTED give the following advice to inspectors.

> Cultural development is concerned both with participation in and appreciation of cultural traditions.

> The school's approach should be active. Inspectors need to look for evidence of how the school seeks to enrich its pupils' knowledge and experience of their own or other cultural traditions, through the curriculum and through visits, clubs and other activities. Aspects of the curriculum such as history, geography, art, music, dance, drama and literature can all make positive contributions, for example, through opportunities for pupils to:

> - visit museums and art galleries;

> - work with artists, authors and performers;

> - develop openness towards and value the music and dance of different cultures;

- appreciate the natural world through art and literature;

- recognise the contribution of many cultures to mathematics and to scientific and technological development.

(Guidance on the Inspection of Nursery and Primary Schools, Office of Standards in Education, 1995)

This guidance could be interpreted as taking a 'national' view of culture. It could lead some schools to think in terms of 'our' culture and 'other country's' culture. There is a more complex view of this whole area, which could be included in an interpretation of this guidance. This view takes account of a range of different cultures existing and interacting within even quite small communities. For example, in music the local culture could include the choral society, the jazz club, the folk group and Radio One, or in the performing arts, ballet, theatre, film or street performers. It may incorporate contributions from English, Scottish, Welsh or Irish, Caribbean, Indian or African cultures. One of the contributors to the culture of every area of the country will be the Christian Church, not least through the music, art, literature it uses in its places of worship and its services.

Somehow the school must provide an introduction and opportunities to explore all of these cultures and many more. No one individual will appreciate or become involved in everything. All should be able to find and develop particular interests and should recognise and value the maintenance and development of traditions that are important in the life of the community or nation.

All four of these areas are important as they acknowledge that schooling is about more than just academic learning and preparation for the world of work. The problems for the schools lie in co-ordinating and resourcing what is taught and in finding the necessary time to achieve all that is desirable.

Concern and care for pupils

A further part of the way in which schools demonstrate their response to the local situation is their concern for their pupils. Many schools become deeply involved in work to help and support their pupils through difficult periods in their lives. They are likely to give considerable time and attention to pupils who

- are coming to terms with tragedy

- experience problems relating to peers or adults

- have difficulties in learning or other special needs including those caused by outstanding ability in a subject or area of learning.

Class teachers or tutors, heads of year and head teachers are likely to be particularly involved in this work but all adults working in schools will have their contribution to make.

In many schools care and concern for their pupils will spill over into care and concern for their parents. It may be that, in some cases, the best way of helping the child is to help the parents. There is a tension here for schools. How much time should they spend helping and supporting parents, when their prime responsibility is to teach children? The challenge may be greatest in areas where there exists considerable social pressure and it is, or seems to be, difficult for parents to contact the other support agencies. Schools are open every weekday during term time. There are teachers and other staff on duty from before nine o'clock until well after four, and there are often staff in the building during holiday periods. Primary schools are usually within walking distance of children's homes. No wonder it seems easier for some parents to bring their troubles to the school than to other agencies whose points of contact may be less accessible.

Worship

Every pupil in every school must attend an act of worship in school every day unless the pupil's parents exercise their rights to withdraw their children under the appropriate conscience clause. This means that even in the smallest school there will be at least five acts of worship each week. In many schools there will be nearer ten and in some large comprehensive schools the number may be more than 150. In county schools the majority of such services must be of a broadly Christian character. In Church schools they will be within the tradition of the church. This implies that the headteachers or worship co-ordinators of most schools are responsible for designing more acts of worship in a week than many priests or ministers, and that without the benefit of a liturgical tradition.

The daily act of worship may be an important opportunity for some children and adults to worship God. For some others perhaps it will be their only opportunity to discover what it might be like to worship. For the rest it will be a time when they have to learn not to interrupt that which is important to others even if they feel unable to participate themselves. The act of worship may also be the time when the school's values are made most explicit to children and to staff. In good schools there will be careful planning of the worship programme and visitors contributing to worship should be aware of how they are expected to fit into the plans. They should also seek to establish some understanding of how many of the school staff and pupils fall into each of the three categories described above as this should influence what they plan to do.

The hidden curriculum

Many men and some women have learnt that sport is so important that they watch it for hours on television and read the back pages of newspapers first. Where and how was this attitude learned?

For many of them it will be the result of learning in school. This is not learning in the conventional sense of having someone set out to teach the concept. It is rather learning absorbed as a result of being part of an institution. We may begin to acquire the attitude that football is a more important issue than life and death by being part of institutions that convey that message by the amount of time, attention and importance that they give to the two issues.

While the content of the subject curriculum is determined by statutory provisions, more is learnt in schools than what is taught in lessons. This learning is sometimes referred to as the 'hidden curriculum'. It is part of the school's contribution to the passing on of national culture and attitudes. Some aspects of this are very good and important. We need to ensure that children are helped to grow up within a society whose better institutions and traditions they understand and value. For example, we all need to help pupils learn that courtesy and concern for others are not optional extras, but part of the basis on which living in everyday society can become tolerable. Most people will regard some aspects of the 'hidden curriculum' as essential and positive. Their views of other aspects, such as the attitude to sport mentioned at the beginning of this section, will differ. Some people may regard one or two aspects as negative. For example, they may perceive the school as encouraging an attitude to male behaviour that suggests that 'big boys don't cry' and find this inappropriate for their own children.

Provision of alternatives

> When he grows up he will be a docker, just like his father and grandfather before him.

This has been an unlikely statement for almost a generation, but there are many equivalent statements which may still have some currency. If it was likely or possible for most children to follow their parents' footsteps then we would probably not need schooling at all. The whole development of school derives from the need to provide a level and range of education for children which can take them beyond their parents' circles of experience and knowledge.

> I have often had cause to be thankful my children were not limited by my lack of knowledge of chemistry or geography. Within the schools that they attended there were teachers who had greater knowledge of and enthusiasm for these subjects than I have ever possessed.

A simple example to illustrate a profound point. If schools exist, in part, to provide alternatives for children and young people then care needs to be exercised over the rhetoric which suggests that 'parents know best'. There is a tension here. Parents should support their own child and his or her interests, but in partnership with schools, not with battle lines drawn.

A further illustration may be useful to stress the importance of this point. For those children entering school at the age of 5 in September 1995, the soonest they are currently allowed to leave school is in June 2006. Their working lives could last until 2055 assuming that retirement stays at the same age as now. Schools are now preparing children for adult experiences into the middle of the next century. The fact requires some considerable thought about what such experiences might be.

> Only just over twenty years ago the electronic calculator was being demonstrated on *Tomorrow's World* as a remarkable new device. The first model cost over £100. If that gives an indication of the pace of change that we have experienced in twenty-five years, for what changes are we preparing our children!

Teachers, parents, governors and all concerned with education need to be joined in a commitment to develop the education of our children for the next century. The Churches have an important part to play in this process as supporters, contributors and partners in the process. The Churches need to ensure that in seeking and accepting such involvement they have an understanding of what schools are required to attempt for their children.

Summary

This chapter has described some of the tasks that face a school today. These include dealing with a range of abilities and experiences, curriculum issues, the spiritual, moral, social and cultural development of pupils, concern and care for pupils and their parents, school worship, the 'hidden curriculum', the provision of alternatives and anticipating the needs of pupils preparing for adult life in the next century. Leading or working in a school is a complex task requiring great energy and professionalism. Churches who are seeking to serve schools need to develop their understanding of all these issues.

Points for thought, discussion and action

- Do we understand the concepts presented in this chapter? If not, how can we be helped to consider them more fully?

- Do we accept the various tasks of the school that have been listed?

- How do these relate to our calling to be the church in this place?

- How can we best help our schools and teachers?

Part II

SCHOOL AND CHURCH

SOME DEFINITIONS

3

The range of schools

W henever a new priest or minister is to be appointed to a Church the congregation should be asked to prepare a profile of the area in which their church is set. This is important in ensuring that the person appointed knows what work is expected of or possible for them. Included in that profile should be details of local schools. For churches who regard engagement with the locality as important, these school details and potential appointees' response to them will be crucial. Where work with schools is a key factor, care should be taken to ensure that potential appointees know this and by their attitude and experience show that they can fulfil this part of their expected ministry.

The descriptions offered in this chapter are designed to help local churches understand the organisation of schools in their area and, as a result, improve their contacts with them. Confusion and irritation can arise if incorrect or misleading terms are used.

> Don't they know that *Playschool* was the name of a television programme?

> Don't they realise that a nursery class and a playgroup are not the same thing?

Inevitably the descriptions are short and do not do justice to the particular types of school, but it is hoped that they will stimulate church people to find out more. All the statistics reflect the position in January 1993 and are taken from the relevant Department for Education and Employment statistical tables and from detailed work done on them at Culham College Institute and published in *The Church of England Schools and Colleges Handbook*, (Culham College Institute, 1993). Note: the figures quoted in this edition of the *Handbook* have been subsequently up-dated. The statistics quoted in this book are from the privately circulated update.

The maintained system

This includes all schools that are part of the State system of education; that is, they receive their financing from the State and education in them is free, although parents and the local community may help to raise money for the school. Within the maintained system, schools may only charge for activities that are not part of the 'curriculum' of the school. There are 22,598 maintained schools in England. These schools provide education for 6,985,753 pupils.

Voluntary

A school within the maintained system which is owned or administered by an educational trust. Most trusts are religious but some may derive from secular bodies such as the City Livery Companies. Voluntary schools are part of the school system that is the responsibility of Local Education Authorities. Almost one-third of all schools in the maintained system are voluntary schools. Of these the majority are Anglican and most of the remainder are Roman Catholic. Some aspects of all voluntary schools must be conducted in accordance with the trust deed of the school. There are 7,238 voluntary schools in England (32 per cent of all maintained schools). They provide education for 1,705,326 pupils (24.4 per cent of those in the maintained system).

County

A school in the maintained system which is not a voluntary school and for which the Local Education Authority is responsible. There are 15,025 county schools in England.

Aided

A voluntary school in which the governors continue to be responsible for the external maintenance of the building and any improvement to it. They receive a grant from the Department for Education and Employment towards the cost of this work. All other payments are made by the Local Education Authority. The governors are the legal employers of most of the staff and are responsible for the admissions policy of the school. Religious Education and school worship are conducted in accordance with the school's trust deed. There are 4,260 Aided schools in England (18.9 per cent of all maintained schools).

Controlled

A voluntary school where the governors no longer provide any financial contribution to the maintenance of the building. The school, while retaining certain aspects of the voluntary school, is controlled by the Local Education Authority who employ the staff and are responsible for the admissions policy of the school. Worship in a Controlled school must be conducted in accordance with the school trust deed. There are 2,978 Controlled schools in England (13.2 per cent of all maintained schools).

Special Agreement

A voluntary school having some features in common with an Aided school and some with a Controlled school. For example, in many Special Agreement schools the Local Education Authority employs the staff but both the Religious Education and the school worship are conducted in accordance with the trust deed. There are 65 Special Agreement schools in England.

Grant Maintained

A school that has opted out of Local Education Authority control and now receives all its funding direct from a central government body (The Funding Agency for Schools). Grant Maintained, sometimes referred to as self-governing, schools may have been county or voluntary and retain some features of their former status. School governors in Grant Maintained schools are responsible for the school admissions policy and employ the staff. They also own the buildings and land that formerly belonged to the Local Education Authority while the school continues. There were 335 Grant Maintained schools in England in January 1993, of which 105 were former voluntary schools. The number of Grant Maintained schools has grown since that date and the numbers in other categories of school have decreased correspondingly.

City Technology Colleges

These schools were created to stimulate the development of high quality science and technology teaching. They receive a proportion of their funds directly from central government but they also have sponsors who have contributed significantly to their initial costs. The sponsors are usually industrial companies. There are 14 City Technology Colleges in England.

Comprehensive

This is a description usually applied to secondary schools which take in children from the entire ability range. Sometimes they may exist alongside grammar schools and therefore only attract a reduced proportion of children with the highest academic ability. Normally they need to be quite large schools in order to be able to provide a range of courses suitable for all abilities. Some 88.5 per cent of all secondary age pupils in maintained schools attend a comprehensive school.

Grammar

These schools select the most academically able children from the area that they serve. The courses provided in them are then designed to enable the selected children to achieve the highest standards of which they are capable. Traditionally these schools served between 10 and 15 per cent of the population. In some areas where only a few grammar schools have been retained, these schools may only be serving the top 2 per cent of the ability range. In many areas they no longer exist. Some 3.8 per cent of all secondary age pupils in maintained schools attend a grammar school.

Modern

These schools provide secondary education for pupils who are not selected for grammar school education in areas where grammar schools take a significant proportion of the total school population. In a few of these areas there may also be Technical schools which provide a technically orientated education for pupils whose abilities suggest that type of education would be appropriate. Some 4.5 per cent of all secondary age pupils in maintained schools attend Modern or Technical schools.

Special

These schools have been created to serve the educational needs of those pupils who are unable to benefit from education in mainstream schools because of their particular needs. Each school usually serves the needs of one or two defined groups of children. For example, there are special schools serving the visually or hearing impaired or those whose behavioural problems are so severe as to make it impossible to educate them with their peers. There are 1,253 Special schools in the maintained system in England.

Nursery

In the maintained sector these schools provide education for children aged between 3 and 5 years old. The majority of children attending such schools do so on a part-time basis. They are staffed by teachers specially trained for the needs of this age group and by qualified nursery nurses. There are 561 nursery schools in the maintained system in England attended by 53,000 children. In the private sector there are nursery schools which may have the same level of staff qualification, but there are also some which are staffed and function in the same way as playgroups. There are no adequate statistics available for the numbers of private nursery schools. Nursery classes attached to infant, first or primary schools have the same staffing rules as nursery schools. Some 286,000 children attend such nursery classes.

Infant

All children must attend school from the beginning of the school term after their fifth birthday, although many will start earlier than this. Unless they enter a nursery school or class, their first experience of formal schooling will be in an infant school or class. Infant schools usually provide education for children aged from 5 to 7 years old. Within the legislation on curriculum issues this age group is known as *Key Stage 1*. This stage of learning lays the foundations for everything that follows.

Junior

These schools provide education for children aged between 7 and 11 years old. For most children this will be the period during which they acquire many of the skills that enable them to face future learning with confidence. They will also begin to develop a wide range of interests. For some children these interests will form the basis for a future career or hobby. Within the legislation on curriculum issues this age group is known as *Key Stage 2*.

Primary

Schools which combine the infant and junior age ranges are referred to as primary schools. In some small primary schools there will be no clear division between the infant and junior stages; indeed, there may well be a class that contains children from both Key Stages. When the education of children under 11 years old is being discussed, it is often referred to as the primary phase of education. There are 18,828 primary schools in England, including all separate infant and junior schools.

First

In some Local Education Authorities the ages at which children transfer from one school to another vary from the pattern in the majority. As the name First School implies, these schools provide education for children between the age of 5 years old, when they enter school and either 8 or 9 depending on the pattern of organisation adopted in the particular Education Authority.

Middle

These schools usually provide education either from the age of 8 to 12 years or from 9 to 13 years depending on the pattern of organisation adopted in the Education Authority. For administrative reasons some authorities have adjusted the age groups in recent years. It is important to check the age range served by middle schools in each different authority where they exist. Middle schools that cater for children up to 12 years old are regarded as primary schools. Those serving children up to 13 years old are regarded as secondary schools.

Secondary

These schools may serve pupils aged from 11 years old to 18, although some may serve a smaller age group depending on local circumstances. The years from 11 to 14 are known in curriculum legislation as *Key Stage 3* and between 14 and 16 as *Key Stage 4.*

High

This name is often given to secondary schools which draw from middle schools and whose intake is, therefore, either 12 or 13 years old on entry to the school. Sometimes the name is also used to describe a secondary school. *Junior High* school is sometimes used to describe a school serving Key Stage 3 only.

Sixth Form College

In some areas pupils transfer from secondary school at the age of 16 to a central college catering for the needs of students between the ages of 16 and 19 years old. Where such colleges offer principally a pattern of academic courses they are known as Sixth Form Colleges. Where they offer a wider range of courses they may be called *Further Education Colleges* or *Tertiary Colleges*. All these colleges form a separate sector of education whose funding comes direct from central government sources through the Further Education Funding Council. In a few areas where there are Sixth Form Colleges some secondary schools have retained their sixth forms and hence provide a range of choices for pupils at this age.

Joint

These are voluntary schools where more than one religious denomination is represented on the trust of the school. There are joint Anglican/Roman Catholic schools and joint Anglican/ Methodist schools. The interest in these schools has been growing as part of the ecumenical movement.

Secular

This is sometimes used to describe county schools, as they have no religious affiliation. There are a few schools in the voluntary sector which have no religious affiliation and therefore are included within the phrase 'secular schools'.

Religious

This is sometimes used to cover those schools in the voluntary sector which have a religious affiliation.

The independent system

This includes all schools to which fees are paid for the children's education. There are 2,249 independent schools in England providing education for 538,000 pupils.

Public

These schools are usually affiliated to the Headmasters' and Headmistress' Conference or the equivalent organisations for girls' schools. They include many of the oldest and most famous schools in the country. All these schools are in the private sector of education. They are usually owned by charitable trusts. Most public schools admit pupils aged either 11 or 13 years old and also to the sixth form. Some have preparatory departments.

Private

These are the schools in the independent sector of education which are not in the Headmasters' Conference. While some are owned by charitable trusts, others may be owned by private proprietors. Some schools in this part of education may be catering for children with special education needs.

Preparatory

Traditionally most of the larger public schools have accepted pupils at the age of 13. Preparatory schools provide education up to this age and specialise in preparing pupils for the entrance examinations of the schools serving the older age groups. Some but not all such schools are linked to a specific senior school.

Special

Some schools in the private sector serve pupils with special educational needs. They may often accept placement of pupils in their school from Local Education Authorities who pay the fees. In some schools such pupils will be in the majority. Some 5,600 pupils attend independent special schools.

Religious

Within the independent sector it is difficult to identify all the schools which have a strong religious commitment. Some have been founded to provide an education that reflects a particular religion or denomination. Such schools would be expected to make that identity clear and to have some form of chaplaincy or its equivalent in place for the school. Other schools may have developed a religious identity as a result of the work of religiously committed teachers or governors.

Secular

Those schools which have no clearly identified religious commitment could be referred to as secular.

Nursery/Kindergarten/Playgroup

There are a number of private nursery schools, kindergartens and playgroups providing an educational experience for children under statutory school age. There is no clear description of each type and all should be subject to inspection by the Local Authority Social Services department to ensure that the premises and other arrangements are appropriate for the age group. Playgroups tend to have high levels of parental involvement in their day-to-day activities. Some private nursery schools may require very little time commitment from parents. Naturally the contribution that parents are asked to pay towards the cost reflects the ratio of paid staff to children and the support in kind or time that parents are asked to make. In some areas the Social Services department may actively support some nursery provision by providing grants or meeting the cost of a proportion of places that are then free to children.

Points for thought, discussion and action

- Which of the types of school listed in this chapter exist in the area served by this church?

- Are we clear how or if they relate to each other?

- Have we people in our congregation who have particular knowledge of these schools?

- How can we learn from these people?

4

The range of churches

I f there is a bewildering range of schools to which churches may relate, there can also be an extraordinary range of churches to which schools may relate. This chapter describes some of them. The majority of Christian Churches are members of the Council of Churches in Britain and Ireland (CCBI) (see Appendix 1, p.93). In addition to the CCBI there are ecumenical organisations for England, Wales, Scotland and Ireland. At the local level there are many ecumenical groups often called 'Churches Together in . . .' or 'The . . . Council of Churches'.

Among each denomination there will be churches which are setting out to be the Christian church for a defined geographical area. While this is the Anglican and the Roman Catholic tradition, many other churches identify with it, not least where there is a shared or inter-denominational church. Other churches in all denominations will be serving a community of members drawn to that church because they value the fellowship, the community care, the style and tradition of worship or the doctrine for which that church is well known. Such eclectic congregations may have a lower commitment to the schools serving the community surrounding the church, but may relate more easily to schools or colleges that also draw from a wide area. For some eclectic congregations their most important contribution to work with local schools will be to support other churches or individuals who do so or to welcome visits from schools whose pupils need to experience the particular tradition of that church as part of their studies in Religious Education.

There will be some churches whose major involvement with the local community will be to present the challenge of the gospel through evangelism. Among their members will be those who preach Christ in the market place and on doorsteps. This is an important ministry conducted in circumstances where people are free to walk away or close the door. It builds on the experience and knowledge of Christians and the gospel story gained by those to whom it is addressed. Its place in schools is within meetings of voluntary societies or clubs. It is not appropriate in the classroom where pupils are required, unless parents make formal objection, to be present or in school collective worship unless undertaken with the full prior knowledge and agreement of the school staff. There may be times when members of such congregations are invited into classes to be asked why they present the gospel in the way that they do. Such occasions are an opportunity to explain 'What my faith means to me and how it affects my life'. They should not be exploited as opportunities to challenge pupils to make their own decision for Christ. Stories that circulate amongst teachers about abuses of hospitality of this type are amongst the reasons why Christians may find themselves viewed with suspicion by schools and may lead in extreme cases to access to a particular school being denied to all representatives of the Christian Churches.

Within the range of Christian Churches that exist in this country there are perhaps five broad groupings with which every child should have had some contact during their programme of learning about Christianity. These are the Anglicans, the Roman Catholics, the Free Churches, the Orthodox and the Pentecostal. Within these groupings there are important differences of emphasis and tradition and, more significantly, much that is held in common. In any area particular denominations or traditions within each grouping may be able to offer particular strengths. By coming to know something about churches within each grouping, children and young people will be helped to:

1. Identify the range of liturgical and free worship used by Christians week by week.

2. Hear the range of music used by Christians in worship.

3. Understand the importance to Christians of the Bible.

4. Gain knowledge of the different ways in which Christians express their sense of community with each other.

5. Appreciate Christianity as a world faith through the variety of links which these groups have world-wide.

6. Identify the different ways in which Christians express their spirituality.

It may be helpful to schools if the churches in a particular area from these different traditions are seen to be working together in their contact with schools and to be mutually supportive in this work.

Points for thought, discussion and action

● Which churches exist in our area?

● Have we an ecumenical organisation such as 'Churches Together in . . .' If not, why not?

● If so, does it co-ordinate the churches' work with schools in our areas? Should it?

Part III

WHAT CAN CHURCHES DO?

5

The essentials

mportant warning to be read and understood by all church people seeking to work in or with schools:

1. The head teacher is responsible for everything that happens in the classroom, in the school and to school parties out on visits.

2. Church members who accept invitations to work in schools are working for the head teacher.

3. Helpers need to be aware of the school's policies and ensure that while they are in the school they conform to them in order to ensure that what they do within the activities in which they are engaged supports and reflects the ethos of the school.

4. Helpers should not be offended if they are asked to complete a form for formal clearance of their suitability to work with young children. This will only be part of routine procedures to ensure that children are as safe from harm in schools as they are in their families or in churches.

If individual church members cannot accept this discipline, work in or with schools should be left to others.

In what follows the phrase 'church ministerial team' is used to cover all those who are in contact with schools on behalf of their church. It is intended to cover the paid priest or minister, if there is one, as well as voluntary priests, ministers, elders, church leaders, leaders of church children's groups and any other member to whom the church has given its authority as a representative. It does not necessarily cover all church members who are parents at the school or who happen to enter the school building.

In the chapters later in this part some suggestions will be made for areas of service that churches could offer to schools. No single church could be doing everything. There are limits to time and energy. The chapters that follow represent more than the minimum that could be expected of any one church. This minimum, however, does exist. There are a number of activities that *all* churches should be offering in service to their local school or schools. This chapter will suggest five distinct activities that every church could and should offer, within an ecumenical framework where possible.

These five activities are:

1. Prayer
2. Befriending
3. Positive support
4. Welcome ministries
5. Freeing members for ministry

1. Prayer

In churches where there is a prayer leaflet each local school could appear on it, preferably with the names and telephone numbers of key staff. This would help develop a powerhouse of private and individual prayer in support of the schools. They should also be remembered in public prayer regularly, not just at the beginning of the school year. A better pattern would be at the beginning and end of each term, on Education Sunday, at examination time in the summer and on the occasion of known special events in school. This would create a pattern of public prayer which would see schools mentioned about once a month through the year, with a special focus in the service on Education Sunday.

2. Befriending

There should be at least one person, preferably a member of the church ministerial team, who knows each school and is known by it as a representative of the church, and is a link between school and church. In most churches the identity of this person will be obvious and the choice natural, but some care is needed to ensure that the person is able to create the positive atmosphere in which further links could be developed.

3. Positive support

Local churches should be supportive in their attitudes in order to help schools in achieving their aims. Staff and governors should know that their work is valued. Teachers, particularly Christian teachers, should be encouraged and their achievements celebrated. Many churches try to do these things but then allow the impact to be damaged by failing to challenge the comment of those who are so shrivelled in spirit that they can only repeat the unthinking criticism spouted by the destructive in our society. Comments like, 'In my day we were taught to read properly' heard when a child stumbles over a word when reading a passage in church or 'Of course the exams are easier now' in response to hearing the achievements of the church's young people, are wrong and deeply damaging – they must be challenged. Left unchallenged, they do the following:

i.   drive youngsters from the church

ii.   hurt teachers who have laboured with pupils to produce the results

iii.   damage the churches' good relationship with schools.

Said by individuals in church the damage may be limited, written by a member of the churches' ministerial team in the local press, such remarks can reduce relations between the churches and local schools to frosty politeness at best.

4. Welcome Ministries

Every church should consider how it welcomes visitors and the purpose for which they might come. Some of the preparation for welcoming could have the effect of making the church more accessible and welcoming to non-school visitors as well.

5. Freeing members for ministry

Some church members may already be giving their time to work in schools or for schools locally as governors, SACRE members, volunteers or members of staff. It does not require much time or effort to ensure that such people know that they have their churches' support for this work. It may take some restraint to ensure that busy people are not forced to choose between their ministry for schools and their ministry within the church. Someone else might organise the church social events in order to free the time of a fellow member of the congregation to maintain their work in schools.

A church that does not do these five things should consider seriously its attitude to schools. A church which is doing these five but no more is probably missing opportunities; that church should study the following chapters to explore what further work might be possible. A church which is doing more than these five things and is co-ordinating their work with other local churches may justifiably claim to be serving their local schools.

Developing relationships with schools

Good relationships between churches and schools are essential. From the church perspective a proper concern for the children in the area that they serve, some of whom will be in contact with the church through Sunday worship or weekday activities, is part of the church's commitment to witness to Christ by service to the local community.

From a school perspective, given that at least a quarter of children are in some form of contact with a Christian Church (Francis and Lankshear, 1988), it will be important for schools to have some knowledge of the experience that children are gaining through their church and its organisations. This is of particular importance in schools where the children give their teachers the impression that 'none of them go to church'. Of course, there will be a few schools where no children are in contact with a Christian church, but these are very few compared with the number of schools who have children who do go to church. Schools will not know whether they really have no children who go to church unless they are in regular contact with the local churches serving their area.

Perhaps the most important first step in establishing good relations between a church and school is to ensure that the staff of the school come to know the church's ministerial team as people. This implies that there should be opportunities when members of the ministerial team can talk with the staff informally, perhaps about mutual interests which will naturally include the children and parents that they both seek to serve and the circumstances in which they are trying to work. Churches and schools have a range of tasks and priorities, some are in common and some of which are complementary, therefore, there exist a number of reasons why there should be dialogue. It is certainly helpful if schools come to understand the work that the churches are seeking to do and, likewise, the churches understand the work of the schools.

Good relationships between ministerial teams and school staff are important but they are not an end in themselves. They are merely the gateway through which a great deal of mutually helpful work can develop once a sound basis has been created.

Points for thought, discussion and action

List the schools in the area served by the Church and for each one list the following:

- Who, in our ministerial team, is involved in promoting our relationships with this school?

- Who in other churches' ministerial teams is involved?

- Is the situation good or does it need more work?

- How can we best contribute to it so that churches and schools benefit?

6

Contribute to school activities

Worship

In an earlier chapter (see page 24) the task of schools in providing acts of worship for every child in the school every day was discussed. Many schools will look for opportunities to invite members of local ministerial teams to contribute to such programmes. However, the contribution could be in the planning as well as in the delivery, and does not necessarily mean that they should be asked to lead the whole act of worship every time they are present. Most schools will wish to plan their programmes of worship with care, and this provides a further opportunity for members of ministerial teams to make a valuable contribution, not least in helping teachers identify the range of worship ideas which are part of the Christian tradition, and which could be used to create a lively programme of school worship.

Not every member of a ministerial team will be good at leading school worship with all age groups. Some may not feel comfortable with any school-age children. No-one should feel compelled to take part if their talents do not lie in this area. Any who do take part must accept that, as with work in the curriculum, when they are in school to lead an act of worship, the head teacher carries the ultimate responsibility for what they do and say. It is very important that they understand that they must operate within the school policy on worship, and that they should be aware of the way in which their contribution has to fit into the overall programme of worship in the school. Much has been written about school worship (Brown and Brown, 1992; Barton *et al.*, 1994), and there is no point in repetition. However, the advent of the arrangements for inspection following the Education (Schools) Act 1992 will lead to many schools seeking to review their policies on worship and the expertise available to them within the local community may be invaluable in the process. Local churches may be able to provide this help, both through the practical experience and expertise of their ministerial team or by putting the school in touch with experts employed by the Church in this field.

It may be that some schools are not aware that many Churches can provide good quality published material which can help the school with its worship. The local churches should be able to bring such material to the school's attention by providing catalogues, arranging displays or lending sample copies. In many parts of the country church organisations can provide training which, by helping people to explore the issues and helping them practise preparing and delivering acts of worship for schools, can build up their confidence and expertise. Local churches should be able to provide information to schools about what is available from their denomination.

Some schools find it difficult to make proper use of help from local churches because of what they perceive as local church rivalries.

> I can't invite Mr Bloggs from the Baptist Church any more, despite the fact that he is brilliant with our children because if I do, I will have to invite someone from each of the other denominations and one or two of them are hopeless.'

This has been said by so many head teachers that it is time that the churches did something about it. The local meeting of clergy or council of churches should be able to identify the gifts that Mr Bloggs has been given by the Spirit in this regard and authorise him to work for them all in taking acts of worship in local schools. If they cannot, what is this saying about the spirit of ecumenism that should exist between them?

School eucharists

In some schools, usually Church schools, it will be right for there to be celebrations of the eucharist. Members of church ministerial teams may have a special part to play in these. Some celebrations of the eucharist may be part of the regular programme of collective worship in the school and, as such, there may be many children and some staff attending the service who are not confirmed or in full adult membership of a Christian Church. Some may not be Christians at all. Many parents, if they are invited to be present, may also not be able to receive communion. Special sensitivity is needed in planning such services. Creative use of the liturgy will be important, as will careful thought about such things as how the administration will be managed. Great care will be needed in such services to ensure that all those who are present are enabled to take part as fully as possible in the service.

In a number of schools celebrations of the eucharist will be voluntary and occur either before school, after school or during the lunch break. They are likely to be attended by committed Christians amongst the staff and pupils and be a focus for prayer about the school as a whole and an opportunity for Christians involved in the school to be strengthened and to encourage each other. Care needs to be taken to ensure that even where the numbers attending are small compared to the number of adults on the staff or the number of pupils in the school, the celebration is part of the life of the school and not separate from it. The prayer focus will be the whole of the school, not just the Christian minority. Church ministerial teams may well be able to contribute to these from their experience of celebrating eucharists for small groups that know each other well.

The celebration of the eucharist in school needs careful consideration, preparation and sensitivity in a Church school. There will be many Church primary schools that do not have such a celebration. In county schools the complexity involved in having a eucharist involving the whole school or a significant section of it will mean that it rarely happens. It is more common to find county schools where there is an occasional opportunity to attend a celebration being held by an informal Christian group or club within the school.

Religious Education

All Religious Education teaching in county and some voluntary schools should be rooted within a planned programme of work related to a Local Authority Agreed Syllabus. In Aided and Special Agreement schools and Grant Maintained schools that formerly had one of these statuses, Religious Education must be conducted in accordance with the trust deed of the school. Usually this will be achieved by following the appropriate diocesan syllabus.

The Local Authority Agreed Syllabus will have been prepared by a conference which consists of four committees representing the

Local Education Authority, the teachers, the Church of England and other Christian denominations or non-Christian faiths. Invitations to join the latter committee come from the Local Education Authority and should be received by the Denominations and Faith Groups in the area. In Wales there are only three committees, as there is no separate committee representing the Anglican Church.

There should be no difficulty for local churches to find out what is expected of them by this syllabus when they seek to support work in schools. They are likely to have had a representative of their own denomination at the conference. That person or a representative of the Local Education Authority should be able to answer questions about the syllabus and how churches can help schools implement it. Churches that are asked to undertake work with a school or class need to ensure that they understand how the work that they will do fits into the syllabus being used by the school.

An essential part of every school Religious Education programme will be the requirement to offer opportunities for children to learn about Christianity as it is experienced today in the Christian Churches (Brown, 1994). Therefore it will be important for church members, and particularly members of their ministerial teams, to be prepared to visit schools to talk about what they believe and how it affects their lives. Sometimes these visitors will be clergy but schools will also wish to call upon 'ordinary' Christians as well. Local churches can help by being willing to suggest suitable local people. Schools will wish to invite clergy in to talk about their work and in some cases to talk about their role in leading worship including, where appropriate, the vestments that they wear.

Teaching and supporting Religious Education

In many churches where there is a paid priest or minister, they may feel that they are expected to make a greater contribution than this to the teaching of Religious Education in schools. Some may expect to be invited to contribute to teaching about the Bible or the story of Christianity. In many primary schools, however, the subject will be integrated into the main timetable, and in all it should relate to the other areas of the curriculum that are being studied in the classroom (Brown, 1992). This may make it difficult to come in from outside to take this subject on its own. Not all priests or ministers will feel confident in their ability to teach young children, and so may be reluctant to become involved with these age groups. Taking a lesson or a series of lessons may not be the most useful contribution that a Christian minister can offer to a school. The development of school policies based on locally determined syllabuses can be a daunting task for a primary school. Few primary schools are able to recruit specialists in Religious Education, and to receive help from a local priest or minister, who should be able to offer insights as a trained theologian and who respects the professionalism and integrity of the teachers, can be of considerable benefit in the task of developing school policies.

In many secondary schools there will a specialist teacher of Religious Education. In such cases he or she will be better qualified professionally to teach the subject than most local priests or ministers. The subject specialist may, however, need help and support in two distinct areas.

1. The demands of the timetable on specialist teachers of Religious Education can often be very high. Not only may they be teaching a full timetable and seeing perhaps five hundred pupils in a week but they may also be supporting non-specialist colleagues who are contributing to the work of the department.

2. As the lone specialist they may find the demands made on them to promote the subject in the school and to maintain its position within the budget, timetable or examination programme difficult to meet in the long term.

The support of local ministers or priests whose academic background may be similar to their own can be encouraging and helpful for such teachers. For all these reasons it may be that for many priests or ministers the contribution to this subject area could be best made in the staff room or with the head teacher, during discussions about the teaching of the subject rather than in the classroom.

Receiving visits

As part of their RE programme schools will wish to arrange visits to local places of worship in order to see what the worshipping community does (other types of visit to local churches will be dealt with later). Therefore it will be important for churches to be prepared to welcome school parties to their church. Many dioceses have produced publications about school visits to churches like *Welcoming Schools* (Church in Wales, 1994).

A checklist for churches preparing for school visits is very helpful.

General

- Hold a planning meeting with representatives of the school beforehand to ensure that the purpose of the visit is clear and agreed.

- Ensure that there is a welcoming individual or group and that they are properly briefed.

- Ensure that the church is clean and warm for the visit.

- If there are areas that pupils are not allowed to enter, are these clearly and appropriately marked?

- Are the locations of the nearest toilets clearly marked and known to the welcome party and the teachers?

- If there are pictures of Saints or heroes of the faith, are their stories known to the welcome party? Are there cards available telling the stories in simple language? Make sure you have enough cards to adequately provide each small group. Don't leave anyone feeling excluded because of lack of cards.

- Do the church notice boards communicate clearly how the church is involved in the local community and linked to other churches regionally, nationally and world-wide? Encourage questions about the work of the Church abroad.

- If there is significant use of symbols within the church building, are their meanings known to the welcome party? Are there cards available giving their meanings?

Specific

- How can we present the church as a lively place of worship Sunday by Sunday?

- How can we best present the way in which the church celebrates its special festivals?

- How can we best present the way in which the church conducts baptisms, weddings and funerals?

- If work sheets are being used by the pupils, is the content known to the welcome group? Who has responsibility for the preparation of the work sheets?

Members of the ministerial team have a particularly important role to play in all of this but they should not ignore the potential for other members of the congregation to contribute. There may be some who can talk simply and well to children or teenagers about the church, what happens within it and why it is important to them.

The National Curriculum subjects

The advent and continuing development of the National Curriculum create a need for schools to be able to call on adults with particular experience or skills to supplement the educational provision for the children (Dearing, 1993). As a result, a range of areas exist in which the churches may be able to provide assistance beyond the field of Religious Education.

This opportunity to support schools may be particularly important in smaller primary schools or in areas where community resources are difficult to identify and use. The range of possible contributions is almost infinite, dependent as they are only on the limitations of the experience and talents that are available inside the church community. In one place the schools may gain assistance with the computer or chess club, in another, extra volunteers to assist on school trips, or someone to contribute to projects or to use their experience in publishing the parish magazine to help the children publish one for their class or school. These activities may not involve members of the ministerial team directly, they may only be the contact between the school and the member of the congregation who has the skills and the time that the school needs.

The children were building a model of a working sailing boat, not a yacht. It had been carefully and lovingly constructed by the children and their teacher. The hull and mast were of wood and the model, five feet long, was almost complete, only the sails remained to be made. These were constructed of paper and carefully glued into place. They looked quite good. One of the sidesmen at the local church was a former fisherman. Visiting the school one day he saw the model. 'It's very good,' he said, 'but the rigging is not quite right and it is a pity that the sails are wrong.' The discussion with the children produced an offer to help. New rigging was constructed and sails were sewn from appropriate cloth. During the work the fisherman's memory was picked clean of stories about fishing and the work done by boats like the one on which the model was based.

While contributions towards the school's teaching programme can help the school, they also create the opportunity for members of church ministerial teams and others to establish good relationships with the children.

Some specific subject areas

Music

There is a great deal of good music teaching being provided in school today. Many parents are paying for their children to receive private instrument lessons. Many churches are using a wide range of talents to provide the music for worship and for other activities. These different opportunities to learn music and to practise music are, in reality, mutually interdependent. It is surprising, therefore, how often schools and churches seem to operate in ignorance of the work that the other is doing. There are many opportunities to build on each other's work if only those involved in church music-making and music-making in school could develop better contacts. This is particularly true of instrumental music-making where churches can often provide experience for children and young people of performing music in company with adults which is potentially very useful in their musical education. Good contacts between school and church could ensure that pupils know that the full range of their music-making is supported in both places.

While it may be the church is using the school's training when it comes to instrumental music, the school may often be benefiting from the experience gained by children from singing in church choirs or music groups. Some schools may be fortunate enough to have a number of children in their classes who are learning to read music through singing in a local church choir and who can therefore form a comparatively skilled backbone of the school choir.

For many schools a visit to a church for any curriculum reason may be enhanced by a musical element. The opportunities for pupils to sing or play an appropriate song may help them to remember the purpose for which the church was built. The opportunity for them to hear the pipe organ, if there is one in the church, and to watch the organist could be a very special experience for young children, particularly those struggling with first stages of piano lessons.

History

Religious Education is not the only subject on the school curriculum where churches may be asked to assist. Many churches are amongst the oldest buildings in their neighbourhood and may contain much evidence of local history or examples of how local people have been involved in national events. Schools may request the opportunity for a class to visit a local church as part of their work in history. It is important that those who will receive the pupils and teachers for this visit know precisely what the pupils will be wanting to study. There is little point in putting the altar frontals on display if the pupils need to spend all their time examining the memorials in the church and the gravestones outside it. If the church has members who are particularly interested and knowledgeable about the history of the building, here may be a golden opportunity to share their enthusiasm with the children.

The Arts

The children attending the local primary school were invited by the local church to design Christmas cards. The most interesting of the designs were printed, with proper acknowledgements, by the church as the front covers for their leaflets about their Christmas services.

A newly created worship centre needed a cross and matching candle-holders for their worship table. The local secondary school was approached. The result of the approach was a simply designed, well-made set appropriate to the context in which they were to be used. They formed part of a GCSE project and were subsequently used regularly in worship.

In the previous section it was pointed out that for a visit by pupils studying history there might be little point in going to the effort of displaying the altar frontals. For many schools their local churches may be the nearest places where the local community's active involvement in the arts is demonstrated. Visits which have sculpture, stained glass, brass rubbing or architecture as their main focus may be much enhanced by being shown the altar frontals or other similar items, particularly if the person doing the showing is someone who is responsible for its care, maintenance or who has had a hand in making some of it. In those churches where the replacement of old kneelers has been an opportunity for valuing local talent there is a further range of possibilities. Not the least of the local talents displayed in churches is flower arranging; while this may not interest all pupils, it is a further example of creativity put to use.

Other curriculum areas

Although three particular areas of the curriculum have been selected so far, there is hardly an area of the curriculum to which a visit to a church cannot contribute. The use of English literature, particularly poetry within worship, is a clear point of contact with the English curriculum.

Every Christian church uses light as a symbol (Genesis 1. 3, John 1. 1-5). Some churches make much of this symbolism visual with extensive use of candles (Paschal candle, Christingles, etc). Others may use pictures that make use of light as a symbol for holiness or for Christ. This symbolic use of light within the Christian church could provide a focus for the Religious Education component of a school theme on light for which the initial starting-point could be an investigation of some of the scientific properties of light.

The links with missionaries, the work of world-wide organisations like the Mothers Union or Traidcraft, the historic or continuing links with other churches at home and abroad may all represent starting-points or points of contact for the geography curriculum.

The wilder parts of a graveyard may offer interesting opportunities for nature study. Some churches have even had conservation centres and nature trails set up in parts of their churchyards.

The important question when a school is planning a visit to the local church for a group of children is 'On what do you wish this particular visit to focus?'. There then needs to follow some careful planning and the involvement of the most appropriate church members in order to ensure that the visit is of maximum benefit to the children.

Remember to make it interesting.

Pilgrimages

For some schools part of their programme of work may include the organisation of a 'pilgrimage' related to the spiritual and moral development of their pupils. This may arise from a historical or religious project on pilgrimages. If this is the case, it will be helpful if, in the context of providing the focus for the journey, the receiving church could provide information or examples of pilgrimages undertaken by church members recently or historically. Some schools may be unaware of the examples in current church life of journeys undertaken for spiritual purposes. Some of these are:

- In Essex there is an annual ecumenical pilgrimage to Bradwell. Similar examples will exist in other parts of the country. Local schools working on pilgrimages should be aware of this event in order to show that pilgrimage is not just an old-fashioned idea, valid only in the Middle Ages, but still has meaning for Christians today.

- A church coach party to hear an evangelist or attend a praise service at a major venue.

- A group from the church attending confirmation or ordination services at a cathedral.

- Visits by church members or church groups to the Holy Land or other important Christian sites.

- Journeys undertaken by representatives of the church to attend a service to mark the commencement of a new stage of ministry of a former leader.

Special events

There are special events in the life of both schools and churches that can bring them together. Sometimes these happen at the initiative of the local church, at other times it will be the school that makes the first move. Some examples are:

- A Suffolk church has a tradition of inviting the local county primary school to attend a service annually on the festival of the Saint after whom the church is named. At the end of the service each child attending receives a bun.

- It is becoming increasingly common for there to be a special service to mark the move of a group of children from one stage of schooling to another or from school to higher education or work. Such services are important parts of these educational 'rites of passage'. Churches can help by providing venues or help in designing and preparing the services.

- At a recent schools event in a cathedral the focus was on the bells which had recently been re-hung after many years of silence. Those pupils attending the event took part in a range of workshops relating to the work of the cathedral with several having an emphasis on the bells. In most dioceses cathedral events have tended to focus on the needs of Church schools, but, in one or two, there is now a growing demand from county schools for such events because they have heard such good reports of them from their colleagues in Church schools.

- In a number of secondary schools those responsible for the spiritual education of the pupils are offering pupils the opportunity to go on retreat or for a quiet day. Churches that provide centres for such activities are clearly providing an important resource. Local ministerial teams should be aware of the retreat houses that are available and may be able to assist or support the planning of the programme for such events.

Voluntary societies

In many schools there is a range of voluntary societies and clubs which enhance the school's life and broaden the education of the children. Some of these such as Christian Unions will be of obvious and direct interest to local churches. Others may only be sustained through the interest and expertise of local church people giving of their time to the school. The parish priest who helps with the football or the computer club or the minister who with a teacher runs a chess club in school are possible examples from a range that is as wide as the talents and interests of the local congregation.

Christian groups: a special case

Many schools, but not all, will have Christian clubs or meetings at lunch time or after school. These are often run by staff and sometimes in secondary schools by older pupils. In many cases the staff involved will not be RE specialists, but will be practising Christians who teach other subjects. Such activities may only occasionally need physical help from local churches, but they should be a focus for encouragement, support and prayer by all the churches in the area.

Points for thought, discussion and action

- What three activities from the range of possibilities could we offer to local schools?

- What activities are we unable to help with?

- How could our people help?

7

Pastoral issues

T here will be times when, if good relations have been established between the church ministerial team and the school, there can be fruitful sharing, co-operation and joint work in the pastoral care of pupils, parents and staff and governors.

Pupils and problems

All schools will be committed to providing a caring environment within which to educate the children. At times this will lead them to undertake tasks that are not strictly speaking part of a teacher's professional expertise. There may be trained counsellors on the school staff, but even so most teachers and support workers, as a result of the quality of their relationships with children, find themselves in counselling roles without the benefits of appropriate training. In a large number of schools there will be staff members who are also involved in supporting parents through crises or periods of uncertainty. The demand for this support arises partly out of the school's concern for the well-being of their pupils and partly because, where parents trust the school, they may see it as the only source of advice locally where the staff are on site and therefore presumed to be available, all day. Many teachers and head teachers feel inadequately trained for the role which is expected of them. A discussion about why the daughter's work seems to be suffering can rapidly change into what feels like a marriage guidance session. It is pointless to say, 'I am sorry I am only concerned with her inability to understand subtraction' when the parent is telling you that her daughter cannot concentrate because she is worried that her father may be about to leave home. Church ministerial team members can make a supportive contribution to this work in several ways.

Prayer

Staff in schools need the prayerful support of local churches in all their work, but especially in their involvement in the care and support of children, young people and their families.

Support

Some church leaders may be able to develop relationships with the staff of the school to such an extent that they are able to provide some more direct support. In particular, they may be able to provide a listening ear for staff who have had to provide help to children or parents with problems which have been traumatic for those individuals to discuss. Naturally, confidences must be respected but talking the issue over with someone who may have relevant experience and who is supportive can be extremely helpful.

Provision of resources

A number of churches publish material on aspects of pastoral care which can be helpful to teachers and others in schools (e.g. Duffy, 1995). Teachers may not be aware of the existence of these resources, and members of ministerial teams may have an important role to play in drawing the attention of staff to these resources and the sources from which they may be obtained.

Direct involvement

This happens only very occasionally. When it does, it will be the school making direct use of the pastoral skills of local church people with whom they have a good relationship. In such cases the church becomes one of the potential reference points when parents or children need more help than the school can give. Naturally, such references can only be made with the co-operation of the parent involved.

'Industrial chaplaincy' for pupils

Pupils also may need the opportunity to talk about their experience in school. This can lead to some delicate areas in church/school relations. Where problems emerge from such discussions they are likely to be in one of four categories.

1. Concerns about progress, examination pressures, options and moves to the next stage of education.

2. Concerns about relationships with peers, which might include issues related to sexual relationships.

3. Concerns about relationships with staff.

4. Concerns about life styles, including drugs, alcohol and other substance abuse.

Attentive listening, reassurance and encouragement are usually all that is needed. Rarely should action be promised or taken and certainly none should be considered that breaches confidences. Considerable sensitivity will be needed when a pupil's concerns reflect criticism of a member of the school staff with whom the listener is seeking to develop good working relationships.

Teachers and problems

The vocation to teach

As with any profession there is a body of knowledge and a range of skills that must be acquired before teachers can be regarded as competent. However, the satisfaction that is gained from the competency in a complex profession is not the reason that most teachers continue to attend their place of work each day. For many a main motivation is a commitment to the children whom they teach. For a significant number their faith in Christ is also part of their motivation. For the Christian teacher, teaching is part of their discipleship and a response to Christ's command to follow Him. A survey, conducted a few years ago, on the background of teachers indicates that there was then a higher proportion of Christians in teaching than could be expected from the number of Christians in the population as a whole (Francis, 1987b).

Nothing concerning the motivation of people to undertake a task is ever straightforward. Visiting a school towards the end of a term and listening to the conversation in the staff room may create the impression that teachers are tired, cynical and only too eager to escape from the profession. This human response to a difficult environment should not blind church people to the real level of commitment within the profession and the significant number of teachers for whom it is still a vocation. Some teachers will have entered their profession with this sense of vocation already developed. Others develop such a vocation through the work that they do.

The churches need to find ways of developing, encouraging and affirming the vocation to teach in the schools in their locality, not only amongst young people but also amongst those who have maturity and experience of the world to offer, as well as other gifts for the children that they will teach.

Nurturing teachers

It is one thing to ensure that vocations to teach are encouraged, it is quite another to seek to support those who are already exercising the Christian ministry of teaching. Work done in churches to encourage the vocation to teach of itself shows the value given to teaching as a ministry, and is part of the support of Christian teachers in the congregation. Nevertheless, most churches will wish to do more than this. One regular opportunity is provided by Education Sunday which is now celebrated by most of the major Churches in this country. This Sunday, the ninth Sunday before Easter, was chosen partly because the theme of the eucharist in the Anglican *Alternative Service Book* is Christ the Teacher. If this Sunday is observed and teachers are regularly prayed for during services, perhaps particularly at the beginning and end of school terms, then the teachers in the congregation will know that there is a concern for them as a group. Christian teachers are individuals, however, and, like most Christians, they will need the opportunities provided by such activities as house groups or meetings with Christian friends to share their story, and to discuss their concerns and worries. Failure to provide such opportunities and to remember the needs of teachers and schools in prayer is a signal that the church is not concerned with them in their vocation.

Unfortunately failing to show care may not be the most unhelpful path that a church can follow in respect of the teachers and potential teachers within their congregation. In some places the congregation are trapped into accepting an idea of the work of teachers and schools that is put about by those who motives are less than honourable. Unthinking, insensitive, ill-informed or destructive criticism of education in general, and the work of teachers in particular, can have a devastating effect on both members of the congregation who are committed to teaching as an expression of their discipleship and Christian teachers in local schools.

There will be some who will argue that this section overstates the case for the support of Christian teachers, but the issue is very important and therefore needs to be energetically argued. Teaching in schools and colleges is not just a matter of exercising certain skills and knowing more about a subject than the group that is being taught. Teaching has important links with the performing arts in so far as the best teachers are able to summon enthusiasm for their topic and convey this to their pupils. To do this they have to be prepared to make themselves open to their pupils and therefore take the risk of becoming vulnerable. The way in which teachers feel about themselves and the task in which they are engaged is vitally important to the quality of their teaching. The morale of teachers is crucial to the success of education. Churches have a duty to ensure that Christian teachers are encouraged and supported in their vocation for the good of the teachers themselves, for the quality of the learning of the pupils and therefore for the value of the witness that they provide.

The above paragraphs have emphasised the importance of supporting the Christian vocation to teach. This should not be interpreted to mean that churches should be interested in or value the work of only Christian teachers. There are many good teachers who are totally committed to their work and the children that they teach who are not Christians. The local Christian church should demonstrate that their right to their own beliefs is respected and that they are valued as colleagues, fellow workers for the children and friends.

The head teacher: a special case?

To have been appointed as a head teacher, a teacher must have demonstrated ability and energy in a number of more junior posts in schools. They will have given considerable time to training and education beyond their initial degree or professional qualification. They are responsible for a wide range of activities in school including many for which their initial professional education will have been an inadequate preparation. One of the unintended effects of much of the recent debate about education has been to lower their prestige and respect in the community while the legislation springing from the debate has increased their responsibilities. Churches must not be tempted to undervalue the importance of the role of the head teacher, nor should they make the common assumption that associates the size of the school or the age of its pupils with the prestige of the post. Some of the most demanding headships are in small primary schools.

Head teachers are often portrayed as the ones who inhibit the development of co-operation, in much the same way the priests or ministers are portrayed as the ones who hold back their churches. The similarity is, of course, that in both cases the responsibility for the administration and organisation depends on them at the day-to-day level. Schools and churches exist for different purposes although they share some objectives. It is not surprising if on occasions the people who carry the responsibility have to say 'no'. This should be understood and accepted. Carrying the responsibility can be a lonely activity, particularly when the traditional support services are being eroded. Good relationships between the church ministerial team and the head teacher may not only facilitate much of the co-operation covered in this book but may also provide part of the support structure that all head teachers need to function effectively.

'Support' staff

In many schools there will be more staff who are not teachers than there are teachers. Many of these people will be active members of local churches, and will bring their own understanding of how their faith affects their life to their work. Often such staff work in posts which carry low status. Dinner ladies, caretakers, cleaners, crossing patrols and school secretaries do not figure in the top ten professions but they are a vital part of the school's work and all of them may have regular contact with children and in some cases parents. Some of them will contribute significantly to the caring work that the school undertakes. The care shown for worried parents by a school secretary can do much to help them express their concerns and receive the help or reassurance that they need. A few minutes observation on a foggy wet morning outside a school, where there is a man or woman employed to help children and parents across a busy street, soon reveals the level of responsibility and occasionally danger carried by such staff. At times of sickness in a school the maintenance of a clean environment in general and clearing up after children have been ill is most important. The responsibility for this rests with the caretaking and cleaning staff. There are some inner city primary schools where the school caretaker not only has to endeavour to keep the premises secure during the night but must also inspect the grounds each morning before the children arrive to ensure that material used and then discarded by drug addicts does not remain in places where children might touch it.

None of the work undertaken by the support staff in school is easy but all of it is responsible. The people undertaking such work need to know that what they are doing is valued by the churches and the local community. Those who are members of our congregations need to feel that the school in which they are working, and their own contribution to it, are supported and upheld in prayer by their church.

Governors

Every school will have at least a dozen governors, some several more. These are people who accept a major responsibility for the policies of the school and the appointment of the staff. They deserve the support of the churches in this voluntary work. Many of them will be a part of the local Christian community. Being a school governor is yet another way that Christians can express their vocation to follow Christ by serving their local community. Christians governors may have a very important role to play in encouraging the links between the school and the local churches. This will not be their only task. They may be able to make an important contribution to the development of policy in Religious Education, school worship, sex education, and the spiritual, moral, social and cultural development of the pupils as well as areas of the general school curriculum where they have insight or expertise.

They may also be able to support those parts of the school's management that are concerned with staff recruitment, selection, development and rewards. They will bring important insights to bear on matters of pupil or even staff discipline. Governors are asked to contribute a considerable amount of their spare time to the role. It is important for churches to realise that one of the ways that they can support members of their congregations who are governors is to free them from other commitments so that they can undertake this service to the school.

Being a governor involves accepting responsibility for the formation of school policy and for the care, as an employer, of the school staff. If a priest or minister accepts the role of governor, there may be times when these responsibilities may seem to conflict with any chaplaincy roles that the ministerial team may also be fulfilling in respect of the school. In such cases it may be important to share the duties between members of the ministerial team if this is possible. Indeed, in a number of Church schools the local ministers are breaking the tradition of accepting the Chair of the governing body and are supporting a lay member in that office in order to facilitate this. The duties of the parochial clergy in respect of the Church schools in their parish, including being an *ex officio* governor in many cases, are such that it is important that, when changes occur, new ministers are aware of the presence of a Church school or schools in the parish, and are positive in their commitment to them.

Parents

Parents, or those who have the parental responsibility for children in their care, have a major role to play in their children's education. This is not just limited to choosing the right schools and then supporting the work of that school. By the example that they provide they are major educator of their children in the home, and there is a limit to what can be achieved at school in areas where children have already learned negative attitudes to schools or learning from their parents. Amongst the possible examples of this is learning to read. A school can teach a child to read, but if there is no example of reading in the home, then it will be much more difficult to enable the child to become a reader who enjoys books for information and entertainment.

Ideally there should be a partnership between the parents and the school in the interest of the child, and much of the school's contact with parents will be designed to foster this partnership. Parents and schools do not always agree, but they should seek to reconcile their differences in order to ensure that their shared goals are achieved.

Christian parents

Christian parents have an important role in setting an example within the partnership between school and parents in general and encouraging the school to meet its spiritual aims. This requires them to take a positive role in the affairs of the school that their children attend. The Church should encourage them in this. Equally, the Church may be taking initiatives to encourage Christian parents to think deeply about their role as a parent in the context of their beliefs. The churches can also provide the support that parents need in the early years of children's lives through the provision of parents and toddler clubs and playgroups. This support for Christian parents provided by the churches' ministerial team will create natural links with schools in the area. Christians parents may be able to facilitate such links.

Christian parents will want to ensure that the school that they choose for their children is a good school in academic and pastoral terms. They will also want to be certain that the spiritual dimension of the school, the Religious Education and the programme of school worship have been given a proper priority in the school's planning and are an important part of the daily life of the school. This should apply to all types of school, not just to Church schools, as these areas of school life are required by law. Therefore when they read about or visit a school that they are considering for their children, they will look for what is said and done about the teaching of Religious Education and the National Curriculum, school worship and the care of the children, as well as the quality of the art work, the number of cups on display, the behaviour and politeness of the children or the impressiveness of the examination results.

Points for thought, discussion and action

- What are we doing to support Christians in our congregation who are involved in local schools?

- What are we doing to support all those working in the schools in the area served by our church?

- How may our work with parents link with that of schools?

8

Sharing activities

Communication

I n any community there will be difficulties in ensuring that accurate information is transmitted about the local community institutions. School gate gossip can be very spontaneous and misinformed. Too often letters carried home by children are processed through the washing machine before they are read by parents. As a result, every school will be looking for ways in which to ensure that its communications with parents are improved. This has become even more important with the publication of league tables of examination and test results. Schools need to develop means whereby the local community knows sufficient about the school's total life to place the league table results in context. Similarly, churches find it difficult to overcome the barriers created by indifference or stereotyped views, when seeking to inform the wider community of their work and activities. There is a clear case for co-operation here.

> Each month the church magazine carries an item from one of the local schools. The item may be a report on the recent activities in the school. It may be some examples of work that the pupils have done. Each school takes it in turn to contribute so that it does not become a burden on a single school and there is always plenty of variety.

Churches should be able to find ways in which local schools can communicate with church members. Exhibitions of work mounted as part of the focus on schools provided by Education Sunday could be one example of this.

Schools could provide opportunities for the local church or churches to let parents and children know about activities and services. Churches could also provide opportunities for schools to let their congregations know about what the school is doing. In many small communities this happens easily and naturally. In larger urban communities it appears to be extremely difficult. Is this because there is less mutual goodwill, or are people not allowing themselves sufficient time to communicate with each other effectively?

Fund-raising

Churches and schools both need to raise funds to support their own activities over and above the contributions of regular members or funds received from the Government or Local Education Authority. It is sensible to suggest that a minimum of co-operation and communication could avoid the worst of clashes and be of mutual assistance. Beyond liaison over the dates and places of events, more could easily be done. Mutual support through publicising each other's activities is a simple and obvious place to start. The school might contribute items to the entertainment at the church fête or concert. The church might provide additional adults, or the use of a hall, for the school's fund-raising activities.

A further aspect of fund-raising which should be mentioned is the charitable giving that is undertaken by schools and by churches. Most schools seek to have a charitable project every term or year. Usually there is a school policy indicating how such projects are to be handled. Most churches have a policy that requires them to give a proportion of their income to charitable purposes outside the parish. Such activities could be mutually supporting. They are certainly activities where good communication could be mutually enhancing. Obvious examples of full co-operation include the school making a collection to support the local church group that is taking a truckload of supplies to Rumania, or the church appealing for its members to help the children collect items to be sold to support famine relief work in Africa. It may even be that on occasions a church and school could agree to work together on a project.

Money management

When financial resources are tight and money has to be efficiently managed, it is important that organisations respect each other's budgets. Schools should be sensitive and aware of occasions when they are expecting churches to support them financially. If, for instance, the school asks to borrow the local church for a concert, has a reasonable sum been offered to cover the costs involved in heating the church? By now churches should have adjusted to the impact of Local Financial Management on Schools. Schools have full responsibility for their own budgets. Therefore, it is not the Local Education Authority which is subsidising the letting of the school hall for the church scout group, but the budget that should be spent on the provision of teachers or consumable material in the classroom. It is important that churches are willing to pay a proper charge for the use of school premises.

This is not to suggest that every aspect of mutual co-operation should have its price or that every offer of payment will be accepted. Much can be achieved by mutual help and co-operation without financial issues being raised. It is important, however, that no-one assumes that the other party has such well-developed sources of funding that it is unnecessary to consider the real cost of requests that are being made.

Contributing to the extension of facilities

Few schools or churches have all the plant and facilities that they need. In some places sharing arrangements, formal or informal, can greatly enhance the work done. Churches may be used by schools for acts of worship, concerts or as place to study aspects of Religious Education, local history or the arts. Schools may be used by churches to provide space for meetings, Sunday School classes or even acts of worship. Taking account of the comments in the financial management section, there seems to be no limit to the possibilities. In some places schools and churches have worked together to provide playgroups or other facilities for the wider local community.

Meeting places

Since many schools do not have large spaces in which to hold meetings, perform or to hold acts of worship, it is not uncommon for such schools to approach local churches with requests for help.

> Can we book the parish hall for a Parents' Association Dance?

Could we hold the carol service in the church because so many parents will want to come that we cannot fit them all into the school hall? In one church in east London there is a school carol service on almost every day of the last fortnight of the Christmas term.

These are opportunities for churches to make schools welcome, to work with them and to build good relationships. Of course, not every request can be met. Certainly some requests will involve costs that the school should be prepared to pay, but all such requests are opportunities for contact and mutual support.

Mutual support

There have already been examples in the preceding chapters of areas where the school may welcome contacts with the local churches for mutual support. Schools and churches that serve the same area should have a close relationship, if only to ensure that they are mutually informed about activities that are being planned or areas of shared concern. These concerns will vary according to local community circumstances. In one area it may be the pressures on family life caused by the local economic situation and the absence of a locally accessible DSS office. In another it may be the problem of children being involved in so many activities in and out of school that careful co-ordination of plans is necessary in order to avoid clashes and the resulting distressed children and irate parents.

Points for thought, discussion and action

- Do we co-ordinate dates of fund-raising with our local schools?

- Do we seek mutual support for special efforts and appeals?

- Do we respect the schools budget when seeking to use their premises?

- Do they respect ours?

- How can we liaise over initiatives to meet local community needs?

9

What about Church schools?

T he Church of England has a long history of involvement with schools in the maintained system of education as well as schools in the independent sector. There are currently 4,864 Church of England schools and 184 Church in Wales schools providing education for around 12 per cent of the children of school age in this country in the maintained system. Most of these schools are primary serving the age range from four+ to eleven but there are also a number of secondary schools serving the needs of older children. There are over 40,000 thousand teachers and 70,000 school governors engaged in providing the education in these schools supported by the Diocesan Directors of Education and their teams. Some of these schools have a long tradition, others are quite recently founded, but most probably have their roots in the last century, even if they are now in modern buildings. Some Church schools have a tradition of serving the Christian community by giving priority in their admissions to the children of church members. Others serve their geographical community by giving priority to the children living close to the school, while others seek to combine both these traditions in their admission policies.

The Roman Catholic Church has over 2,100 schools serving 9.8 per cent of children of school age. There are probably 33,000 teachers and 25,000 governors in Roman Catholic schools in the maintained sector. They are supported by the diocesan teams for schools and for Religious Education.

The Methodist Church has 30 schools in the maintained system serving 0.1 per cent of the children of school age. A small but growing number of Church schools are ecumenical in their foundation, being funded jointly by more than one church.

Every Church school represents a considerable commitment in time and money on behalf of the local church community to enable it to continue in existence. Such a commitment is rewarded by the pastoral contacts that it provides for the church with the children and their parents and into the wider community and the opportunity that it gives to influence by example the work done in other schools in the area. The benefit to the parish of having a Church school has been demonstrated by recent research findings (Francis and Lankshear, 1993) and the appreciation of the role of the Churches and their schools in the education system of this country by the Government is demonstrated by the frequency of reference to it in the recent White Paper *Choice and Diversity* (HMSO 1992).

How do Church schools provide Christian witness?

Church schools provide a witness to Christ by the quality of the service that they provide to the community and the way in which they make their motivation for this clear. Therefore it is important that they are good schools, and that no-one can be in any doubt that they are Church schools. Such schools will demonstrate that they have a clear understanding of what it means to be the Church school in the location in which it is set (Brown and Lankshear, 1995). This implies that the worship and the Religious Education are excellent and that the relationships within the school and between the school and members of the wider community are founded on the teaching of the gospels (Lankshear, 1992). At a more mundane level there should be clear signals in the school and outside it that this is a Church school. No-one should be left in any doubt on that score. This does not mean that there should not be sensitivity to and respect for the feelings of parents and pupils from other faiths, but, rather, that such sensitivity should not involve a Church school in apologising for its Christian foundation.

The worshipping community and the Church school

The worshipping community that has a Church school has an important privilege and responsibility. It benefits from the opportunities that the school provides to show its care and concern for the people living in the parish through the provision of high quality education for the children and through the opportunities for contact that the existence of the school creates. Of course there are costs in terms of money and time, and it is to be hoped that neighbouring churches will wish to be helpful and supportive in meeting such costs, but the potential rewards in the long term outweigh the short-term problems. In many parishes the school buildings also represent a major asset in the church's pastoral and social work outside school hours where this is compatible with the primary purpose of the building, which is the provision of education in a school context. Support for the school should be more than worship. Finance, prayer, time and talents need to be committed in this great work of education.

Churches that have Church schools have a particular range of tasks which need to be undertaken in support of them (Duncan and Lankshear, 1995). These include:

1. Chaplaincy – supporting the pupils and staff of the school to contribute to the worshipping life of the school and its Christian ethos.

2. Government – providing a number of people including the priest or minister to be members of the governing body whose work includes all aspects of:

    *   employing staff

    *   developing policies

    *   managing finance and buildings

    *   possibly administering admissions

    *   aspects of the school's discipline procedures.

3. Funding – most churches will contribute to the costs of supporting the school on a regular basis, including making provision in their budgets for regular donations. In all Church schools this will provide some finance to support the aspect of the Christian character of the school. In Aided and Special Agreement schools it will also contribute to the governors' share of the costs related to the school premises.

4. Work with parents – being involved with the Parent/Teacher Association or its equivalent and knowing parents and their children so that the school may be able to respond to their needs.

5.   Being involved in Community and Local Education Authority networks, i.e., governor training activities, LEA officers, etc.

6.   The parish priest and some of the lay officials of the church may be involved as trustees of the school building and any money or other property held on trust for the school.

The priest/minister cannot do all of this alone. He or she will need help and support, for every church with a Church school there needs to be careful prayer and thought before it is decided what tasks the priest/minister will take and what will be done by other church members. There are no rules, except that it is very rare for the priest/minister not to be on the governing body. Tradition only helps if it helps. In many Church schools the priest/minister is the Chair of the Governing Body. This is tradition and it is helpful if one of the church governors is the Chair but it should only be the priest if that is the best use of everyone's time and talents.

For most churches that have a Church school there will be at least five or six church members, including the priest or minister, who are giving significant time to support the school. They in their turn need support from the church.

From time to time the church council will have business to conduct in relation to the school. They cannot do this effectively if they never hear about the school at other times. There should exist well-developed ways for the council to hear about the activities of the school and the governors via reports or items for discussion. This will ensure that, for example, when the church council receives a copy of an inspection report from OFSTED on the work of the Church school, they will have a basic knowledge and understanding with which to receive it.

One way of establishing such links is for the head teacher of the school to be an *ex officio* member of the parochial church council. In some areas when a new head teacher is appointed to work in a Church school the church holds a special service to commission the head teacher for this Christian ministry.

Points for thought, discussion and action

- Are there church schools in the area served by this church?

- At what cost, financial and human is the church's involvement being maintained?

- How can we help?

10

Supporting the work of the Churches amongst schools and teachers at regional and national levels

I t should not be forgotten that many Churches have regional and national organisations that are active in education. Regionally, the Anglican and Catholic dioceses are active in their support of work in schools, and many other denominations will have resources available at this level.

Sometimes ecumenical organisations are able to sponsor school workers for an area, perhaps working with the support of the Scripture Union or another similar agency. Where such workers exist, it is important that their brief is clear and that they are enabled to relate effectively to other Christians already involved with the schools locally or regionally. Their tasks need to be carefully defined. Requiring them to relate to schools using several of the models of work mentioned in the first chapter of this book may lead to confusion or disappointment when assumed objectives are not met.

Nationally, in the Church of England, the General Synod Board of Education and the National Society are the means whereby the support for the work of Church schools, Religious Education, school worship and Christian teachers are resourced and given a focus. For the Roman Catholic Church equivalent work is done by the Catholic Education Service. Other denominations have their own structures and these meet together nationally through the Churches Joint Education Policy Committee, which is related to Christians Together in England. Ecumenical bodies that work to support schools include the Scripture Union and the Christian Education Movement.

A particular national initiative by the Churches Joint Education Policy Committee which can help local churches in their work with schools is Education Sunday. This takes place every year on the ninth Sunday before Easter. Materials for the event are developed ecumenically but published by individual denominations in ways that are appropriate to their own traditions. It provides an opportunity to celebrate and pray for the work of schools and colleges. It can be an opportunity to make the whole congregation aware of the close relationships that have been developed between the local churches and local schools.

While no local church should be unaware of how its own denomination or the Churches working ecumenically support work in schools, it is the role of the local church in supporting Christians involved with education and the Christian institutions that continue to thrive within the education system that is of vital importance if the Church is to continue to make a full contribution to the education system into the next century. It is a task for every church, even if there is no Church school and no teacher, governor, educational administrator or even child in the congregation. Prayer is important, practical and moral support is vital and financial support is crucial and every church can give these.

Points for thought, discussion and action

- Do we know what our church is doing at regional and national level in education?

- How are we making this work known to local schools?

- Is there a local schools worker?

- Do we know what this worker is doing?

- How are we supporting this work?

11

Exercise to assist reflection on Part III

I n this part a variety of different areas have been suggested as possible opportunities for developing links between local churches and schools. It is possible, but unlikely, that some churches may be able to identify work that they are doing with schools within each of the chapters. Most churches will have recognised some activities that they have already established with some schools. What follows is designed to promote reflection by church members and leaders on the pattern that exists within their own church, measured against the range of possibilities in the preceding chapters.

Review Chapter 1 and decide which type or types of church most closely describe your own. Your church may have some of the characteristics of an 'evangelical', 'shrine' and a 'supporter', or an 'Anglican' that is 'open all hours'.

Having decided which categories most closely match your own church:

- Choose three activities from Chapters 6 to 10 which you think would be most appropriate for your type of church in your area.

- Choose three which would be least appropriate.

- Identify any of the activities that you know that your church is doing.

- What do your answers suggest that your church should do now?

Part IV

CONCLUSION

12

Everyone cannot do everything

I n the last part a range of possible ideas for action were explored. No church acting on its own could possibly do everything. No school would want all these things done. Choices have to be made between possibilities. Most of these will be determined by local factors – what are the pressing needs? Where do our talents lie? What resources do we have available? Some choices will be made because they are simple, obvious and essential. These form a basic minimum which the local churches in an area acting together should be able to provide for every school.

The minimum action kit was discussed in detail in Chapter 5. The main headings were:

1. Prayer

2. Befriending

3. Positive support

4. Welcome ministries

5. Freeing members for ministry

No church that is doing all these things should feel guilty if it is not doing more. More may be possible and desirable but only where resources, people and time but not necessarily money, permit. If only one of these five is possible, then it must be prayer. If there is prayer, it is unlikely that in time it will be the only one.

Working in the service of local schools should not be a chore or a duty but it should be a joy and a privilege. It is so exciting to be involved in helping children and young people to grow and learn, no-one should begrudge being involved. Of course, there are frustrations. Children are not perfect. Young people can be and often are adolescent in all the negative meanings of that word. There are, however, also joys:

- Sharing in the successes of individuals and schools.

- The laughter when things go right or when they end in spectacular failure.

- The joys outweigh the frustrations.

We know that we are serving Christ in serving schools and the pupils in them. What greater joy could there be than that?

Appendix 1

At the time of writing the following churches are members of CCBI:

The Baptist Union of Great Britain

Cherubim and Seraphim Council of Churches

The Church in Wales

The Church of England

The Church of Ireland

The Church of Scotland

Congregational Federation

The Congregational Union of Scotland

The Council of African and Afro-Caribbean Churches

The Council of Oriental Orthodox Christian Churches

Independent Methodist Churches

International Ministerial Council of Great Britain

Joint Council for Anglo-Caribbean Churches

Lutheran Council of Great Britain

Methodist Church

Methodist Church in Ireland

Moravian Church

New Testament Assembly

Presbyterian Church of Wales

Religious Society of Friends

Roman Catholic Church in England and Wales

Roman Catholic Church in Scotland

Russian Orthodox Church

Salvation Army (British Territory)

Scottish Episcopal Church

Union of Welsh Independents

United Free Church of Scotland

United Reform Church

Wesleyan Holiness Church

Appendix 2

Useful addresses

The General Synod of the Church of England,
Board of Education
Church House
Great Smith Street
London SW1P 3NZ

The National Society
Church House
Great Smith Street
London SW1P 3NZ

The Catholic Education Service
39 Eccleston Square
London SW1V 1BX

The Methodist Department of Education and Youth
Chester House
Pages Lane
Muswell Hill
London N10

The Department for Education and Employment
Great Smith Street
London
SW1P 3BT

Your Diocese or regional church organisation (write in)

Your LEA (write in)

References

Anonymous (1994) *Welcoming Schools* (Penarth: Church in Wales).

Barton, D., Brown, A and Brown, E. (1994) *Open The Door* (London; The National Society and Oxford Diocesan Education Services).

Brown, A. (1992) *Religious Education* (London: The National Society).

Brown, A. (1994) *Christianity in the Agreed Syllabus* (London: The National Society).

Brown, A. and Brown, E. (1992) *Primary School Worship* (London: The National Society).

Brown, A. and Lankshear D.W. (1995) *Inspection Handbook for Section 13 Inspections in Schools of the Church of England and Church in Wales* (London: The National Society).

Culham College Institute (1993) *The Church of England Schools and Colleges Handbook* (Redhill: The School Government Publishing Company). The figures quoted in this edition have been subsequently updated. The statistics quoted in this book are from the privately circulated update.

Dearing, R. (1993) *The National Curriculum and its Assessment* (London: School Curriculum and Assessment Authority).

Duffy, W. (1995) *Children and Bereavement* (London: The National Society).

Duncan, G. and Lankshear D.W. (1995) *Church Schools* (London: The National Society).

The Education Act 1944 (London: HMSO).

The Education Reform Act 1988 (London: HMSO).

The Education (Schools) Act 1992 (London: HMSO).

Francis, L.J. (1987a) *Religion in the Primary School* (London: Collins Liturgical).

95

Francis, L.J. (1987b) *Partnership in Rural Education* (London: Collins).

Francis, L.J. and Lankshear, D.W. (1988) *Children in the Way* (London: NS/CHP).

Francis, L.J. and Lankshear, D.W. (1993) *Christian Perspectives on Church Schools* (Leominster: Gracewing – Fowler/Wright).

Her Majesty's Chief Inspector of Schools (1995) *Guidance on Inspection of Nursery and Primary Schools* (London: HMSO).

HM Government (1992) *Choice and Diversity* (London: HMSO).

Lankshear, D.W. (1992) *Looking for Quality in a Church School* (London: The National Society).